What Therapists Say and Why They Say It

What Therapists Say and Why They Say It

Effective Therapeutic Responses and Techniques

BILL McHENRY
Shippensburg University of Pennsylvania

JIM McHENRY
Professor Emeritus
Edinboro University of Pennsylvania

PEARSON

Boston   New York   San Francisco   Mexico City   Montreal
Toronto   London   Madrid   Munich   Paris   Hong Kong
Singapore   Tokyo   Cape Town   Sydney

Executive Editor: Virginia Lanigan
Series Editorial Assistant: Matthew Buchholz
Senior Marketing Manager: Kris Ellis-Levy
Composition and Prepress Buyer: Linda Cox
Manufacturing Buyer: Linda Morris
Manufacturing Manager: Megan Cochran
Cover Administrator: Linda Knowles
Editorial-Production Coordinator: Paula Carroll
Editorial-Production Service: Publishers' Design and Production Services, Inc.
Electronic Composition: Publishers' Design and Production Services, Inc.
Chaper opening cartoons: Lisa K. Walker

For related titles and support materials, visit our online catalog at
www.ablongman.com.

Library of Congress Cataloging-in-Publication Data
McHenry, Bill.
    What therapists say and why they say it / Bill McHenry, Jim McHenry.
        p. cm.
    Includes bibliographical references and index.
    ISBN 0-205-48477-8 (alk. paper)
        1. Psychotherapy. 2. Psychotherapists. I. McHenry, Jim. II. Title.
RC480.M394 2007
616.89'14—dc22   2006040871

Printed in the United States of America

10 9 8 7 6 5 4 3 2 1   11 10 09 08 07 06

Contents

Preface

We have provided therapy to those in need in a myriad of settings (schools, colleges and universities, rehabilitation settings, programs for students who are disadvantaged, etc.) and have taught aspiring therapists in graduate school, collectively, for fifty plus years combined. Along the way, we have consulted with many helping professionals and attended many skill-enhancing workshops. Those experiences, coupled with the basic question learners sometimes pose, such as "Can you give me an example of that?" led us to write this book.

Though we have seen many books throughout the years addressing clinical skills, we thought there was a significant gap. There was no book that cataloged, described, and provided examples of many of the techniques, basic and advanced, used in therapy. This book is our attempt to fill that gap.

Of course skills and techniques alone cannot make a successful therapist or therapeutic session. As one of our mentors (Bill's), Dr. Frank Main, professor of counseling at The University of South Dakota, is wont to say, "the therapist enters the room when the technician leaves." We firmly agree with Frank.

We hope this book will be used by therapists-in-training to broaden and enhance skill development, by counselor educators to augment and supplement student learning, and by practitioners to continue to expand their therapeutic repertoire.

Acknowledgments

We would like to thank the professionals at Allyn and Bacon for the space and production assistance they provided for our vision to come to life. Special thanks go to Virginia Lanigan and Scott Blaszak for their encouragement, guidance, support, and enthusiasm for the project.

You made the process enjoyable and relaxed while providing us with timely information and critical editorial comments.

We thank Lisa Walker for her professional illustrations that brought to life the images we had in our heads.

This book could not have arrived without the keen eyes of Dr. Bradley Will, Fort Hays State University, and Linda McHenry, MA. Their painstaking diligence in helping edit and critique our work enabled us to significantly improve the book.

Along the way we needed technical assistance in preparing and editing our manuscript. Our thanks go to Nick Walker for helping us navigate our way through the technological quagmire. Your expertise and patience are much appreciated.

We are eternally grateful to our students who provided us with the gift of the original seed for this book. Without their desire to continually grow professionally and develop their clinical skills, we would not have heard the catalyzing question, "Can you give me an example of that?"

Along the way, we received feedback and necessary constructive criticism regarding this project from many students. We thank them for taking time to provide that invaluable assistance.

We thank our colleagues both past and present—your voices are reflected in our work.

Throughout the process, our independent reviewers provided useful and critical information related to the structure, writing style, and manuscript language. Their efforts helped us strengthen the book in a number of significant ways.

Finally, we want to thank Paula McHenry and Melissa McHenry for their love and support along the way.

What Therapists Say and Why They Say It

CHAPTER 1

Welcome

So you're going to be a therapist. Welcome! Congratulations on joining a group of professionals who work every day helping people deal more effectively with many of the issues they face in their daily lives. Therapists play an ever-increasing role in our society, and in that role they help clients work through a variety of concerns; some are positive, such as assisting someone in making a choice among several attractive alternatives, and some are negative, such as working with substance abuse or the death of a loved one.

Chances are you're choosing this career because you've been told that you're a "good listener." It's likely you were one of those people in high school or in your dorm to whom others poured out their troubles. Experiences like that have probably already taught you one of therapy's larger lessons. Being able to unload a burden to a listening ear can be a real help to a person experiencing genuine pain in her life.

As you were listening, however, you may have been simultaneously processing several of your own reactions. While feeling very honored that another human being was demonstrating such real trust in you by sharing very personal and deeply meaningful emotions, you may have also felt a growing anxiety within yourself, possibly bordering on panic, because you simply didn't have a clear idea of just what you should say or just how you should react. You may have felt that you were in "over your head." Maybe one of the reasons you appeared to be such a good listener then was that you simply had no idea how to respond to this person's pain. That feeling probably taught you another very basic fact about therapy: *A therapy session, whether conducted in an office or outdoors sitting on opposite ends of a log, is not a simple conversation.*

While being a good listener may be an important and necessary prequel to many forms of therapy, listening, in and of itself, is usually not sufficient to help the person change behavior.

So what else do you need? That's a great question—an important question. However, as with many of the great and important questions scientists—including behavioral scientists—deal with, the answer is not easy to come by. In actuality, the answer depends on whom you talk to. Consider the many theories extant on how to hit a baseball, how to kick a field goal, how to win an election, or how to treat a patient. Then recognize that many of these "accepted" theories actually contradict each other. Medicine offers us clear examples of such contradictions. An extreme example is a branch of medical practice that relies on poisons and toxins to attempt to *cure* patients—not a mainstream therapy. Another example is Christian Scientists' almost exclusive dependence on prayer to heal patients—again, certainly not mainstream. Similarly, therapy literature is filled with many suggestions regarding how this thing called *therapy* should occur. Some of these suggestions may actually appear to be contradictory. For example, Adlerian therapists are taught to ask clients to recall early recollections (from before the age of eight). Solution-focused therapists, on the other hand, focus attention almost exclusively on the present and future, avoiding as much as possible any efforts the client makes to discuss his childhood.

Therefore, in the final analysis *there actually is no final analysis.* Instead we have a number of hypotheses, theories, suppositions, and the like, suggesting that there is more than one way to skin the proverbial cat. Maybe then, just as there is more than one way to hit a baseball, kick a field goal, win an election, or cure a patient, we must conclude that there is more than one way to engage in the therapeutic relationship. This brings us to the matter at hand.

Purpose of the Book

Our goal with this book is to help both therapists and therapists-in-training as they develop, expand, and refine both their skills and their understanding of the practice of therapy. As such, we wrote the book as a direct response to students who pose the basic question: "Can you give me an example of what that might sound like?" While those students understand the words used in the literature, they continually push their professors to provide concrete examples. Their questions are specific:

"How do you get a client to focus on the here and now?"
"How do you define a problem?"
"How does confrontation work—exactly?"

This book has been designed to be straightforward and to the point. It presents over one hundred different skills, techniques, and ways of conducting the therapy interview. Yet the coverage, of course, is not comprehensive. Therapy is an ever-growing and dynamic field.

What Is Not Here

The dynamics of personal therapy involve two or more unique human beings interacting in the moment. In this shifting and dynamic landscape, no exact, rigid "lesson plan" is possible. Therefore, some cautionary observations are warranted regarding several important therapy components that you will not find covered in these pages. Indeed, we firmly believe you will not find them in any book.

Perhaps most important, *you will not find your own sense of authenticity*. While you may read over and review each skill, really incorporating those skills and techniques may be difficult. Such acquisition will be determined partly by your own comfort level and will depend partly on your own working theory of how this "therapy thing" works. Being authentic in the moment requires a certain degree of trust in the techniques and skills you are using. If you lack that trust, both the client and the therapy process may suffer.

What you make of the material contained herein will also be shaped by your own values, beliefs, and worldview. If, for example, you hold tight to the notion that a therapist should not provide any direction at all for the client—that the client should find her own way of life—you may not connect well with the skills used in the *Directive technique.*

As you wrestle with attaining greater skill in therapy, understand that you will make mistakes. Perfectionism is as unattainable in this field as in any other. Doctors attend their patients' funerals. World-class chefs burn the soup. Great hitters in baseball fail to hit more than two-thirds of the time. You get the point. No one has ever conducted a perfect therapy session, but practice and feedback will make you a better therapist. You will benefit from experiences such as audio- and videotaped sessions, role plays, and both live and post hoc supervision.

Of course, and maybe most important, clients vary. Some enter therapy genuinely committed and determined to change (about one-half of the clients you might meet in marriage therapy, for example); others are just as firmly resistant (think about therapy conducted with clients who are incarcerated or the resistant half, and sometimes both, of the clients you might meet in marriage therapy, for example). Each and every client enters with a different personality, demeanor, worldview, and attitude, which are added to and merged with a dozen or a thousand-dozen or so other personal characteristics.

Obviously, working with this truly unique individual (different from any other person on the earth!) requires the full attention of the attending therapist. And, significantly, when this unique human being is immersed in the therapy process, an in-the-moment process, the relationship itself becomes a dynamic, shifting, changing landscape for both the therapist and the client as they proceed by fits and starts through the thickets toward greater client insight. Therapy is definitely not rigid. Consequently, progress rests on the quality of the interaction that occurs between the therapist and the client(s), and that interaction is shaped, for better or worse, by therapeutic decisions (direction or lack of same, tone, etc.) made by the skilled therapist. One size does not fit all.

Implementation of some of the skills in this book requires great care on the part of the therapist. "First, do no harm," must be more than a just a slogan for the therapist. For example, harm can result if the therapist tries to *Externalize the Problem,* causing the client to focus blame and responsibility for the problem inappropriately (and counterproductively) on another person or people. Using the *Spitting in the Client's Soup technique* before the therapist has developed adequate rapport with the client is another example. In the latter situation, the therapist may not only hurt the therapeutic relationship, but may also leave the client wondering if all therapists are so cruel and mean-spirited.

What Is Here

- 106 therapy skills/techniques
- 1,395 therapist responses
- 2 partial fictional transcripts utilizing the skills presented in the two chapters that focus on many of the basic listening skills
- 1 full transcript utilizing the skills described in the book
- 9 sets of practice exercises
- 10 examples of intertwined interventions
- 31 annotated references for further skill and theory development

So, take a look. The material includes basic therapy skills such as *Open Question, Closed Question, Minimal Encourager, Reflection of Meaning, Reflection of Feeling, Paraphrase, Empathy,* and *Immediacy*. Beyond these basic skills is a multitude of others that you might also consider adding to your personal therapy practice. No matter which skills seem to work best for you, provide the greatest comfort level for you, or best fit your philosophy of human behavior, you should push yourself to continue to grow in your clinical skills. So, if you're a .300 hitter this year, why not try to move it up to .310 or .320 next year! The material in this book can be practiced through your entire career as a therapist. You can visit and revisit skills as you work with new clients, and you may find that you are continuing to develop new and clearer ways of seeing and hearing people.

Layout of the Book

For each skill presented in this book we provide the therapy approach the skill is most closely aligned with (individual, family, group, cognitive-behavioral, etc.). We include a brief definition of the skill along with a statement that gives you a sense of how to incorporate it. Finally, we provide examples of each skill. These examples were created by us from our work as counselors and counselor educators and from our observations, supervision, and consultation with other therapists (fifty plus years combined).

Without a doubt, there are many ways to utilize these skills. The examples offered in this text were written from the authors' perspectives, although an attempt was made to utilize different types of "therapist voices" in the examples. It should be clearly noted that each therapist will find his own way to integrate the philosophy and technique associated with each skill. For example, one therapist may be very direct and to the point in asking the client for information, while another may "blow on the embers" of a piece of the client's story to uncover the same information.

We arranged the skills in chapters that reflect natural groups gleaned from both historical and current therapy texts. We reviewed individual, group, play, couples, and family therapy and included as many different skills as possible. We also consulted various theoretical models for this book.

Chapters are not isolated by clear boundaries. In fact, several skills could be, and were, considered for several different chapters. Additionally, as you read each skill definition, you may notice that words or phrases in the definition also seem to fit other skill definitions. For example, one could argue that the following therapist comment could be considered both a *Paraphrase* and a *Reflection of Feeling:*

> *Client:* I really feel bad about this situation
>
> *Therapist:* You feel terrible about the situation.

Obviously, the therapist has reflected a similar feeling as described by the client, while also reflecting back, in different words, the content of what the client said. Thus, the definition of both skills has been adequately met. No one has ever said that therapy is an exact science.

Of course, perhaps one way to discern whether this response was either a *Reflection of Feeling* or a *Paraphrase* might be to actually hear the inflection in the therapist's voice. If the therapist placed emphasis on the word *terrible,* one could argue that she is highlighting for the client that the feeling was understood and focused on. If, on the other hand, the therapist had placed no greater inflection on any of the words, it may simply be a paraphrase.

We are taking the time to point this out now because factors such as the power and presence of tone of voice, tenor, pace of speech, use of silence, and pauses along with other nonverbal behaviors on the part of the therapist *do* have a major impact on the message being sent to the client. Consider a second example. This time we will use a one-word response by the therapist that may fit the criteria of several different skills found in this book.

> *Client:* I am really feeling like I am alone in life right now.
>
> *Therapist:* Lonely(.) or (?) or (.)

That one word—*lonely*—may mean a number of things to the client, each of which is dependent on the therapist's response (tone of voice, inflection, and associated affect) and the client's interpretation. If the therapist adds inflection to the end of the word, it may sound like an *Indirect Open Question*. If the therapist uses no affect or inflection, it may be a *Paraphrase.* If the therapist shows affect that might lead the client to believe the therapist understands what feeling lonely is about, it could be either *Empathy* or *Reflection of Feeling.* Finally, if the therapist uses a nonverbal response that is confrontational, this could be considered an indirect form of *Confrontation.*

So as you read the following pages, clearly recognize that it is not simply words that make up the skill. Factors such as timing in the session, affect generated by the therapist, vocal qualities of the therapist as the message is delivered, and, of course, ways the message is perceived by the client may all be extremely important. Such nonverbals really matter. The way you sit, the way you gesture, your facial expression, and the tone, pitch, and volume of your voice are all important components that impact the quality of the interchange between and among you and your client(s).

As an example, consider how you felt the last time you noticed that a person you were talking to was preoccupied in thought about something else. You may have been going on and on about last week's football game, while your spouse was wondering if she really had made an appointment with the physician. How did you arrive at the realization that you didn't have her full attention? Or any of her attention? Was it the flat affect "um hum . . . right . . . I understand" responses, or did her eyes and body language communicate more clearly than words that she was focused on something other than what you were saying.

With all these variables in play, of course, mistakes will occur. They are unavoidable. You will make mistakes (or what's a practicum for)? Although we cannot offer any blanket suggestions of how to totally eliminate such errors, we have included several nontherapeutic "techniques" to avoid. For example, think of a time when you were having a major problem in your life and *you* needed someone to really listen and provide counsel (it does, in fact, happen to everybody). While you were experiencing that pain, that crisis, did anyone say, "Just don't worry about it. Things will turn out all right. Don't think about it," or some variation of the same theme? Although inspired by good intentions, this seemingly kind sentiment is merely a Band-Aid offered to soothe a person until somehow, someway (maybe magically) healing takes place. This is advice giving. Advice giving is usually ineffective and is often counterproductive (e.g., forget, banish, suppress, repress). It is not therapy. Consider your own experience. Were things suddenly all right? Did you say to yourself, "Okay, I will not worry about it." Or did you turn to someone else for help in dealing with the pain? Almost anyone can give advice. Therapists attempt to give assistance. There is a large difference.

Enhancing Skill Development— Theory into Practice

Extracting individual skills, even for the sake of discussion, and suggesting that they fit here and not there is a difficult (possibly impossible) task, because many theories overlap in goals, intentions, and, of course, skills. For example, Adlerian-based clinicians attempt to arouse a new cognitive awareness in the client through making once-covert beliefs and messages overt. Rational Emotive Behavioral Therapists do something similar.

Further complicating the attempt to pull out individual skills is the fact that different therapists using the same skill may arrive at very different responses to the client depending on the goals of the theory base. An *Interpretation* by a psychoanalyst may be anchored in strengthening the ego, while an interpretation of the same client material may be reframed for the positive intentions of the client by a brief therapist.

Having stated that, what does seem clear, however, is that to be most effective in using therapeutic techniques, a clinician must have a strong sense of his own unique personal theory. This technical eclecticism combines the teachings of various and varied theories to form a unique and consistent personal theory of therapy, which then proves effective for the individual clinician. The following section reviews some of the more highly publicized and widely accepted clinical theories.

Psychoanalysis   Credited to Sigmund Freud, this approach relies heavily on the clinician's ability to interpret and analyze the stream of material produced by the client. Every word is considered and weighed for both overt and covert meaning while the client talks through early life experiences, current situations, or anything else that comes to mind. The clinician's role initially is to create a safe setting for the client to express internal thoughts they had never known existed or had never shared with anyone. From this new material, one of the main goals of psychoanalysis can be achieved. The clinician can successfully interpret and accurately analyze the material to help the client acquire a newly informed sense of her personality.

There is no doubt that psychoanalysts use many of the skills in this book. *Interpretation, Minimal Encourager, Prompt, Paraphrase, Technical Expert,* and *Providing Feedback* are several of the skills most commonly used by these clinicians.

Individual Psychology   Credited to Alfred Adler, this theory base views the purpose of the therapist as one who aids in the further development of the client's positive lifestyle (roughly equates to personality). To do this, the clinician uses techniques that help the client acquire a greater sense of social connection, while placing less emphasis on overcoming her self-perceived inferiorities.

Through the creation of a warm and safe therapeutic environment, the individual psychologist enlists the cooperation of the client in interpreting and analyzing pieces of his lifestyle. In doing this, the Adlerian therapist may utilize family and community resources.

Skills in this book that are directly aligned with Adlerian individual psychology include *Minimal Encourager, Paraphrase, Reflection of Feeling, Reflection of Meaning, Interpretation, Accent, Empathy, Closed Question, Open Question, Asking the Question, Miracle Question, Reframe, Metaphor, Spitting in the Client's Soup, Providing Feedback, Early Recollections, Acting "As If,"* and *Directive.*

Humanism/Existentialism   Credited to Carl Rogers, Rollo May, and Viktor Frankl, this approach has the clinician focus on promoting answers to client questions from within the client. This is accomplished by creating a safe, nonjudgmental place for the client to express and interpret her own material. The therapist helps the client assume more responsibility for her thoughts, feelings, and behaviors while attributing her own meaning to life events.

To do this, the therapist uses techniques that focus on creating the right space for the client to decide to make changes for himself, and very little on the therapist directing movement. These skills include *Empathy, Minimal Encouragers, Paraphrase, Reflection of Feeling, Reflection of Meaning, Summary, Prompts, Accent, Checkout, Here and Now, Defining the Problem/Issue, Defining Goals/Objectives/Outcomes,* and *Self-disclosure.*

Gestalt Therapy   Credited to Laura and Fritz Perls, this theory encourages the clinician to help the client become more fully aware of self while focusing on the experience of the moment. In doing this, the client learns to more readily be aware of her behaviors, body language, and awareness of surroundings.

This theory base is strongly rooted in the moment. Thus, skills and technical components emphasize the current situation—both the one presently being held by the client and the one presently existing between the therapist and client(s).

Skills in this book that closely align with Gestalt therapy include *Closed Question, Open Question, Probe, Forced Choice Question, Here and Now, Changing Questions to Statements, Clarifying the Purpose, Confrontation, Observation, Affirmation, Immediacy, Creative Imagery, Empty Chair Technique,* and *Role Playing.*

Cognitive/Cognitive-Behavioral Therapy   Credited to Albert Ellis, William Glasser, and Aaron Beck, this approach strongly suggests that the client is in charge of both his thoughts and behaviors. By learning to assume such responsibility, the client then gains awareness that he is in charge of creating and/or maintaining the problem. Therapists who use this theory base actively and energetically analyze the comments and story of the client for thoughts and behaviors that are not consistent with one another, are not rational, and/or place blame for one's misery or discomfort on someone else.

In this book, many skills can be used readily by these clinicians. Some of the more prominent in this theory base include *Downward Arrow, Closed Question, Open Question, Cognitive Disputation, Triadic Questioning, Collaborative Empiricism, Capping, Confrontation, Providing Information, Progressive Relaxation, Imaginal Treatment, Self-monitoring, Shame Attack, Stop and Monitor, Bibliotherapy,* and *Homework.*

Family/Systems Theory   This broad theory base is credited to many individuals. Among its core tenets is the belief that there is no direct linear cause of a problem. Instead, problems are created and maintained by the entire system to create balance within the system, maintain complimentary relationships, and at times help other systems function more effectively.

Though diverse in their nature, and having distinct ways of intervening using therapeutic techniques, the general techniques in this book that align most closely with family/systems theory include *Circular Questioning, Process Illumination, Blocking, Reframe, Compliment, Interpretation, Metaphor, Redefining/Reframing, Observation, Confirmation, Immediacy, Self-disclosure, Holding the Focus, Drawing Out, Joining, Camera Check, Conjoint Family Drawing, Directive, Door-in-the-Face Technique, Foot-in-the-Door Technique, Paradox, Self-monitoring, Ordeals,* and *Homework.*

Brief Therapy   Credited to many past and current theorists, this approach focuses substantially on solutions to problems rather than the cause or root of the problem. The active and engaged therapist looks for opportunities in the client's story to add missing pieces that may lead the client to either think or act differently in relation to the problem. The clinician helps find the missing pieces by surfacing exceptions to client rules, and by helping the client see the problem as a problem and not see themselves as the problem. Skills in this book that align with brief models of therapy include *Metaphor, Asking the Question, Miracle Question, Externalizing the Problem, Forced Choice Question, The Terrible Question, Scaling Question, Reframe, Compliment, Providing Information, Directive, Paradox, Ordeals,* and *Homework.*

As you advance in your own personal skill development, you will naturally begin to define your own therapy style. You will no longer aspire to be like Rogers, Ellis, or Adler. That's entirely appropriate, because what you will become is an authentic therapist, a professional therapist, who uses bits and parts of many theories and approaches you have gleaned from the heavy hitters who have preceded you in the field. You will not slavishly follow some blueprint, and you will not be a mere composite. You will be a therapist with an integrated and eclectic theory and practice of your own.

In that growing process, the individual skills in this book will become ever-more accessible to you, and you will find it easier to link such skills together in your therapy. For example, rather than simply paraphrasing what the client said, you may find that linking your paraphrase with an open question will be more productive in the therapeutic interaction.

As an aid to such skill acquisition, the chapters on therapy skills are followed by a brief chapter called Intertwined Interventions, which provides examples of how various skills and skill sets can be and are put together to facilitate client growth, therapist understanding, and a more therapeutic relationship. In the final two chapters we offer practice exercises and an annotated list of references reflecting many of the current and past therapy texts on therapy skills.

We genuinely hope that you enjoy the book and find the material useful as you develop into a competent professional therapist. Our goal is both to define and provide concrete, specific examples of a wide range of skills currently in use in the field of therapy.

Once again, congratulations and welcome!

CHAPTER 2

Pragmatic Therapy

Organization of the Chapters and Skills

The major underlying assumptions that form the foundation of this book and provide the bases for pragmatic therapy are the following:

1. Therapy works.
2. Therapists need to be equipped with as many skills as possible in order to effectively meet the needs of each of their various and unique clients.

3.   For some clients, simply being heard is necessary and sufficient; for others changing fundamental thinking patterns is necessary; and for others actual behavior change is necessary.

With this foundation in mind we offer the following pages as a guide—a broad conceptual framework—to how the skills and chapters fit together.

In a pragmatic sense, therapy consists of three tiers. The first tier is where the therapist hears how the client sees herself in the moment. This can be accomplished by using skills primarily found in The Reflecting Pool and The Questioning Tree chapters (Chapters 3 and 4). For some clients the seemingly simple action of having a skilled therapist really listen to them can be very therapeutic in and of itself. In fact, in some cases, this is all that is needed for a client to make a change and regain her psychological, cognitive, emotional, and/or spiritual equilibrium. Of course, in most other cases, listening is simply not sufficient.

Often, as rapport and increased therapist-client understanding develops, the process moves on to the second tier. Skills that can be helpful here are found in the following chapters: The Framework, Looking for Clear Skies, Chasing Down Mirages, The Supply Line, Therapist's Actions, and Pure Imagination (Chapter 5–10). Through such skills, the therapist helps the client get to a more useful cognitive place. Through imagined changes, feedback from others, and confrontation of thoughts and behaviors, among others, the power of the mind and change of thoughts in itself can heal. For some clients, this will be all they need to continue moving in a more positive direction. Still others may need more help.

The third tier is the place where the therapist and client focus on actions rather than just words, thoughts, or feelings. *Waves in Motion* (Chapter 11) offers skills used to effect such possible remedies. The use of these action-oriented skills helps the client actually change behavior(s) rather than simply talk about it or imagine it.

Note that each of the tiers has both a distinct set of principles and a distinct purpose in the therapy process. Though seemingly linear in nature, in reality, effective therapy may require the therapist to revisit techniques and even earlier tiers at various times during the therapeutic relationship. For example, therapists may continue to use reflections, even when prescribing action.

Consider the following fictional account as a way of possibly anchoring the basic tenets of pragmatic therapy.

Story of Pat

Alone and isolated on a deserted island, Pat wished very much to be rescued. Time had slowly passed, it had been several years since arriving. Though Pat had no recollection of how things came to be, a glimmer of hope survived day by day. There had been natural desert trials and tribulations that tested Pat's ability to remain intact—testing the realms of psychological, emotional, spiritual, physical, and cognitive fortitude. Through it all Pat kept moving, kept hoping for life to change, to improve.

Then one day, another soul arrived on the island. Pat gave the visitor fair space for several days. Then, out of curiosity or pain or need or something else, Pat finally decided to greet the visitor.

Seeing the two together would have been very telling: the stranger with new clothes, no sunburn, smelling fresh and clean, Pat smelling of the island scent, patches of skin showing the tell-tale signs of burns, both old and new, unkempt hair, clothing tattered. Realizing this, Pat asked for a mirror. Not having one, the stranger suggested the two of them walk over to the nearby pool of water to see their reflections. Nervous and a bit apprehensive at first, Pat took a look. Surprisingly, though looking quite different in cosmetic ways, the pair seemed to share a common resemblance that they both noted. "Not so bad," Pat said. The stranger agreed.

Desiring to get out of the sun, the stranger then suggested that the two move over a few feet to sit under the shade of a tree. As they sat, they talked. Pat shared parts of her island story; the stranger asked questions trying to get an ever-more complete picture. All the while, they alternately gazed at each other and at each of their reflections in the pool.

Out of the corner of the stranger's eye, something emerged that had not been noted previously—a primitive camp site. The stranger noted the sticks, twigs, and branches strewn about haphazardly as if to resemble a cot, noting also the broken palms and leaves assembled in a crudely simple structure. Knowing that at times actions are more powerful than words, and seeing that Pat needed some help in assembling a more useful frame, the stranger walked over to more closely inspect the island palace. Then, with Pat's permission, the newcomer began to assemble a much more substantial frame for both the sleeping quarters and shelter.

Together, the stranger and Pat moved from the tree to the pool to the newly fortified framework, talking and sharing as they went.

Though much of the conversation revolved around Pat's experience on the island, and the current experience they both were having, the stranger became less strange and more known by supplying information to Pat as it was needed. As their relationship continued, Pat felt growing confidence in sharing her story.

Day turned into night and the pair shared comfort and safety under the newly erected frame. Then, almost simultaneously, they began to notice the overwhelming number of stars in the night sky. Coupled with the full moon, the night sky illuminated the island, its two inhabitants, the tree, the frame, and the pool. Pat commented that the same sky had never, since her arrival on the island, seemed as clear and beautiful.

Late into the night, still talking, immersing themselves in the pool, the tree, the solid frame, the clear sky, Pat suddenly jumped up and yelled, "Did you see that?" The stranger had not. A short time later, Pat shrieked, "You must have seen that then?" Again, nothing was there to be seen. The stranger queried Pat, "What did you see?" Pat, sheepishly at first, told the stranger story after story of "things" that appeared and seemed real but defied explanation. They both had to chuckle when Pat said, "Late last week I saw a fish jump out of the water and tell a bird to stop fishing in her territory. Then the bird responded by saying that the fish was too nosey, and they would have to seek the counsel of the secretary of state, which was a giant octopus."

The stranger said, "Of course the octopus ruled in favor of the fish, the bird claimed nepotism (but distant cousins don't count)." Though they both laughed, the stranger knew that this had really occurred in Pat's mind. They took time to process such a unique mirage.

The next morning the two picked up on the previous day's discussion. Still sitting by the pool, tree, frame, under clear skies, chasing away mirages as they surfaced for Pat, they began to discuss what they could see as the best situation on the island. They talked about how things could be at their best, even in such a difficult situation. Through pure imagination, Pat and the stranger played games in the mind that allowed for a creative interplay of what was real and what they would have liked to be real. For lunch, Pat imagined a steak sandwich with fries and the stranger had pizza and a salad. Pat felt energized.

The stranger then noticed that all they were doing was talking. Though the conversation was good, they were no closer to either getting off the island or having a better place on it. After some gentle persuasion, Pat agreed to venture on a trip around the island. Off they went. On the far side of the island, the stranger stopped and peered out to sea: "Do you see that?" Pat asked, "What?" The stranger, pointing out to the horizon, replied, "There's a giant shoreline with buildings, lights, cars. I can even see people moving around." Pat quickly remarked, "You can see that too?" It was no mirage.

Quickly the two worked to build a safe and secure craft to navigate the unknown waters. Setting off, they noticed that the motion of the waves propelled them along. Seemingly faster than a motor boat could go, the two arrived at their destination quickly.

Parting ways, the two reflected on how their journey had changed the both of them. The stranger noted that Pat had showed the resilience, internal strength, and courage to keep going while alone on the island, even in the face of such strong negative forces. Pat reflected on learning how, if ever again seemingly stranded on a deserted island, she might search for ways—sometimes closer at hand than one might think—to get off the island.

The categories we offer as cornerstones to pragmatic therapy, found both in the previous story and in the following chapters, allow the therapist to envision alternative skills and approaches when working with clients. In some cases, it may take longer to help a client "see" himself in the reflecting pool, while another client may need very little time to start the initial reflection process. Yet the latter client may need help with his frame, mirages, or clear skies aspect. As each client brings different strengths, so too will each therapist have strengths in certain areas (e.g., questions, supplies, waves in motion).

As we noted earlier, this book contains over one hundred different skills, techniques, or ways of conducting therapy sessions. Those methods are separated into ten chapters, although the partitioning may sometimes be viewed as arbitrary. Of course, the resultant divisions and structures are designed as guideposts that we hope will be useful in helping the therapist continue to develop and refine her own personal theory and practice of counseling.

CHAPTER 3

The Reflecting Pool

With each of the skill in this chapter, the therapist employs some variation of reflection of the client's words, feelings, meanings, and/or thoughts. This pool of skills assists the therapist in establishing rapport with the client. By accurately reflecting back what has been said, the therapist clearly indicates that she understands what the client is really saying. Obviously, productive reflection involves a key and most basic principle of therapy—active listening. Routine parroting of the client's words and overuse of this technique are obviously counterproductive.

Minimal Encourager

Approach aligned with: Universal skill

Purpose: To encourage continued discussion by the client without interrupting or changing the focus.

What the therapist does: The therapist uses general encouragers (e.g., "uh huh") or words and phrases specific to what the client is saying (e.g., "painful," "happy," "unforgettable").

Examples:

1. okay
2. uh huh
3. stuff
4. chores
5. the end of the night
6. I hear you
7. I'm understanding you
8. I see
9. I feel you
10. right
11. happy
12. painful
13. please continue
14. oh, okay
15. hmmm
16. I get it
17. keep going
18. oh, okay, I see
19. right, right, okay
20. angry
21. breathless
22. arrogant
23. continue

Client: I find myself waiting for her to make the first move, but, I don't know, I feel bad about the situation.

Therapist: (silence accompanied by a head nod). *or*

Therapist: Okay, I hear you. *or*

Therapist: Uh huh, okay. *or*

Paraphrase

Approach aligned with: Universal skill

Purpose: To show the client that the therapist is listening by reflecting or giving back the message the client has said in somewhat different words. The meaning, tone, feeling, and content of the client's message are maintained. The therapist acts simply as a backboard for the client to hear her own thoughts in a new way.

What the therapist does: The therapist selects a few of the client's words that stand out from other things the client has said and repeats them back in a different way to the client.

Examples:

24. You have a lot on your plate.
25. You have a number of things to do each day.
26. There are a lot of things that you have to get done each night.
27. You are responsible for doing a lot at work.
28. Your coworkers treat you like you are less important than them.
29. If I hear you right, you are saying that your coworkers ask you to do a lot of things for them.
30. You are sometimes responsible for things that are not really your job.
31. You do work for others, don't get credit for some of your work, and are at times treated as a lesser member of the organization.
32. You are not sure what you are actually responsible for.
33. Pete started a fight that led to you getting in trouble.
34. You didn't start the fight that got you in trouble.
35. You got in trouble for fighting.
36. Getting into trouble is not new for you.
37. You seem to get in trouble frequently.
38. Mike started the fighting and you got into trouble, which happens a lot.
39. It sounds like you didn't start the fight.

Client: Yesterday my mom told me that we are going to do things different at home from now on.

Therapist: You found out yesterday that things are going to change in your family. *or*

Therapist: Your family is changing. *or*

Therapist: Suddenly, things are going to be different in your house.

Reflection of Feeling

Approach aligned with: Universal skill

Purpose: To show the client that the therapist is aware of the feelings involved in the story, words, and language of the client. The therapist also uses this skill to connect with the client on an empathic level.

What the therapist does: The therapist highlights for the client what the client has said (e.g., "I feel mad!" "You feel angry."), and, without changing the meaning, presents it to the client using either the exact same or equivalent feeling word or words (e.g., "mad" = "pissed off" = "upset" = "angry").

Examples:

40. You feel like you are being pulled in several directions.
41. You are under a lot of pressure.
42. Right now, your life is pretty stressful.
43. You are worn out by the end of the night.
44. By the end of the night, you are exhausted.
45. You feel a bit overwhelmed by all of your duties.
46. You must be tired.
47. It sounds like you are a bit overworked.
48. All of those duties can be a bit overwhelming.
49. You are under a lot of stress and pressure.
50. You feel a lot of pressure to do many things at work.
51. You feel underappreciated.
52. There is a sense of being taken for granted.
53. Your coworkers don't understand your need for clarity.
54. At work right now, there is a lot of stress and pressure.
55. Going to work is difficult.
56. You feel like you were being attacked.
57. That had to be a bit confusing.
58. You feel like getting into trouble is not that big of a deal.
59. It sounds like you feel exhausted by the end of the day.

Client: It is really painful to talk about it, but, yeah, I was really pissed off about having to change jobs.

Therapist: You feel angry about this. *or*

Therapist: It really hurts to talk about that time of your life. *or*

Therapist: You are upset about what happened.

Reflection of Meaning

Approach aligned with: Universal skill

Purpose: To show the client that the therapist has heard and understood the deeper meaning to the story. This deeper meaning is usually a core belief that guides the client's actions or principles. In most cases, the Reflection of Meaning is adding new information for the client.

What the therapist does: The therapist listens to the story of the client and then gives back in a direct statement what he has heard as the core beliefs, attitudes, or assumptions that the client is expressing indirectly.

Examples:

60. One of your core beliefs is that if you don't do something, it won't get done.
61. Sounds like you really value doing things for others.
62. If you didn't do all of those things, they would never get done.
63. Your needs are less important than the needs of others.
64. No one takes the time to really help you.
65. Others don't care much for your needs.
66. One of your core beliefs is that some people need to be taken care of.
67. You mean that things are not fair.
68. The rules of life are hard to figure out.
69. People don't pay close enough attention to you.
70. Others take advantage of you.
71. If allowed, other people will take advantage of you.
72. Your coworkers walk all over you.
73. Things are up in the air right now.
74. Your work is about projects, you would like it to be more personalized.

Client: It really makes me mad that I did that. I could see Wendy and David acting like that, but not me. I mean, I should not have been so stupid—I know better than that.

Therapist: So, if I understand it right, you believe that you should be perfect even when those around you fail. *or*

Therapist: You believe you should see things more clearly than those around you.

Downward Arrow

Approach aligned with: Cognitive-Behavioral therapy

Purpose: To identify and bring to the surface the core beliefs an individual holds.

What the therapist does: The therapist uses reflections and questions to get from a superficial belief to a core, underlying belief. The therapist keeps the focus on the underlying belief of each statement made by the client.

75. As we have talked, I have heard you say several times that you feel as though you and others see you as a strong person. I wonder, what does that say about you, "being a strong person"? (client responds) If that's true, that you are never hurt by others and able to always take care of yourself, then what does that mean to you? (client responds) So then, you believe deep down that to show weakness is a sign of being imperfect, and you must always be perfect.

76. You are saying that you feel that you are stupid if you fail another test. I am curious what being stupid means to you? (client responds) Then, if that's true, that being stupid means others will see you as incapable, then what does that say about you? (client responds) Right, okay, then that says you are more concerned about what others think than what you believe about yourself. Then that tells you what about yourself? (client responds) That means you are only of value if others see you doing things right.

77. So I understand you saying that your parents and doctor think you have ADHD. I am curious, what does that mean to you if it is true? (client responds) Okay, then if that is true, that you are not normal, what does that mean to you? (client responds) Okay, then I hear you saying that that means you are not a good person.

78. **Therapist:** I understand what you are saying, that you believe you should do more for your three-year-old son. I wonder, what it means to you that you must be a better mother to your son?

    Client: *I have to keep him safe.*

Therapist: Okay, then what does that indicate about you that you must always be there for him to protect him and keep him safe?

Client: *Mothers are judged by how well they protect their kids.*

Therapist: All right, then finally, what do you hear about yourself when you say you must not be seen by others as a poor mother?

Client: *If I don't keep him safe, others will look at me as a failure.*

Therapist: So you are worthless if you are not a perfect parent.

Summary

Approach aligned with: Universal skill

Purpose: To capture a general sense of the discussion over an extended period of time. Therapists may use summaries to start a session, cover material from previous sessions, during a session, and at the end of a session to help the client see what ground has been covered and what topics have been discussed.

What the therapist does: The therapist makes a statement that captures the essence of what has been talked about over an extended period of time (either in that session or over several sessions).

Examples:

79. So in summary, what I heard you talk about this session includes your strength and resiliency to the demands of life, the loss of your grandmother, how to handle grief and what you would like to see yourself doing differently in the future.

80. As we start this session I wanted to revisit what we discussed last week—we talked about how drugs and alcohol have affected your family, and in particular, you; we discussed the cycle of abuse, and we touched on, right at the end, some of the ways that you have been able to cope with such a challenging time in your life.

81. You have given me a lot this session. Let me take a minute and recap some of what you have said. You said that you have difficulty enjoying sex, and that your boyfriend would like you to move in with him. You also said that you remember some aspects of being abused sexually as a child. Did I miss anything?

82. It seems to be a natural place in the session to summarize what we have discussed thus far. You have covered several aspects of your life, including difficulty maintaining employment, weight issues, feeling depressed, and having no clear direction in life.

83. As our time runs out this session, I want to cover what you have shared this week—that being, you're worried about your mother and her new boyfriend, you don't really care if you pass tenth grade or not, and you are unsure of what you want to be when you grow up.

84. Just to recap, we have talked about career options, jobs you have had in the past, and what you are looking for in a career.

Child's Content of Play

Approach aligned with: Play therapy

Purpose: To verbally highlight the child's own behavioral actions for him. It is also used to maintain contact with the child in a noninvasive manner.

What the therapist does: The therapist describes what the child is doing as the child is engaged in therapeutic/metaphoric play. It is a play-by-play description of the action—highlighting the child's actions, behaviors, and sometimes intentions. Care must be taken by the therapist to allow the child to name the objects or show exactly what they are through play.

85. You are working hard at that puzzle.
86. It looks like you are drawing a picture of your family.
87. You are laughing hard.
88. You have stopped coloring and now are cleaning up the markers.
89. Now that you have found the puppet you like, you are playing with it.
90. You are making someone out of that clay.
91. You've decided to arrange the toys in order of height.
92. You and your sister are playing with the sand box.
93. You're making a picture of your family.
94. You are looking around at the toys and objects in the room.
95. You are hitting the ball.
96. playing with the star man
97. Now you're banging the drum.
98. You are organizing.
99. You see something in the corner.
100. You are laughing.
101. You are shooting with the gun.
102. making bread
103. looking around the room
104. You have found something you like.
105. taking your time
106. going faster now
107. watching me work
108. You are building a sand castle.
109. Now you have gone to the shelf to get something else.

Child's Feelings

Approach aligned with: Play therapy

Purpose: To make overt and highlight the feelings of the child while she is engaged in play.

What the therapist does: The therapist makes direct statements while the child is engaged in play that capture the feelings being expressed by the child. These therapist statements are not made to have the child respond or stop play, but to offer a play-by-play of the child's apparent emotional state.

Examples:

110. You are upset about the crayon breaking.
111. It looks like you are happy when you talk about your family.
112. You are really happy to see that toy again.
113. It makes you feel sad when we have to stop playing in the sand.
114. You are worried about how all the animals will get along in such a small place.
115. You are not happy with the way the lion treats the giraffe.
116. It sounds like you are happy to be meeting with me again.
117. You look confused by the new arrangement of toys on the shelf.
118. It makes you feel upset when other kids take your toy.
119. You are mad about the fact that we don't have a red crayon that works.
120. You feel confused that that doesn't fit.
121. It is fun to play.
122. Making pictures is difficult.
123. Coloring is something you really enjoy.
124. You're tired.
125. You feel excited that you found where that piece goes.
126. You are sad about not being able to play with that.
127. It is exciting to find new toys.
128. Looking outside on a rainy day makes you feel blue.
129. When your mom leaves the room it can be scary.

130. Being around so many toys and things to do is a lot of fun.

131. Drawing a picture of your family makes you happy.

132. Putting a puzzle together is difficult.

133. That is really hard work.

134. You are feeling very good about what you made.

135. It looks like you are excited and happy to see what you accomplished.

Accent

Approach aligned with: Universal skill

Purpose: To maintain discussion along a similar path or line of thought.

What the therapist does: The therapist highlights the last few words spoken by the client to keep the same train of thought going. The therapist gives back to the client the exact words that the client just spoke in a way that encourages further exploration along the same line.

136. making you mad
137. are very upset
138. makes you think it is time for a change
139. is hard
140. lots of people do it
141. cannot imagine it any different
142. frustrated
143. feel a strong connection
144. moving in the right direction
145. have a lot to do
146. interested in finding out more
147. unsure what to do
148. really love to be around them
149. feeling overwhelmed
150. tired
151. happy about the outcome
152. scared to be alone
153. feels like a lot
154. testing the waters
155. angry about it
156. happy for them
157. excited about the change
158. unsure what to do
159. know what you want
160. have faith
161. can't imagine it
162. was a really good time

Client: I am really excited about this weekend.

Therapist: . . . excited about this weekend

Empathy

Approach aligned with: Universal skill

Purpose: The therapist shows the client through words or actions that she understands what the client is experiencing.

What the therapist does: The therapist communicates to the client that she is hearing, feeling, and understanding the core components to the story when she reflects back to the client that the deeper meaning in the client's message has been received.

Examples:

163. That must have been terrible to watch your mother die.
164. It must be very gratifying and empowering to do that.
165. You must have a strong sense of being alone.
166. In your story it sounded like you were talking about guilt, fear, and anxiety.
167. I get the sense that you are torn apart by such actions.
168. You must have been horrified to hear that.
169. It must have been troubling to get that much feedback in that moment.
170. Right now you are very alone.
171. As you have shared your story I have been touched by the notion of you feeling as if very few people really care about you.
172. You have had enough pain and torment in your life.
173. That must have been terrifying.
174. I can imagine that to have been an amazing experience.
175. You must have felt like your world was crumbling.
176. Your heart must have been touched by that comment.
177. No one sees how hard you work at that.
178. For you, life takes a lot of work and effort.
179. It took courage to say that to your mother.
180. It must feel good to have so many people who care about you.
181. Your family doesn't notice how hard you work.

Client: When I think about it, I guess I have never talked to my wife like that, you know, I never asserted myself in that way.

Therapist: You must have been nervous and apprehensive about doing that. *or*

Therapist: You are struck by the strength you showed in that moment.

Prompts

Approach aligned with: Universal skill

Purpose: To help the client either add to his or her story or continue talking about the same thing in more detail.

What the therapist does: The therapist encourages continued discussion either by asking the client to talk more about something or by highlighting the last few words said by the client.

Examples:

182. Could you tell me more about that?
183. I am interested in hearing some more along those lines.
184. It seems that there is more to the story.
185. Please continue.
186. Okay, so what else can you add to help me understand the story?
187. Would you be able to give me more information about that?
188. I'm not sure I fully understand, you said hurt and angry.
189. Can you tell me more about what happened?
190. I'm hearing you.
191. I understand what you are saying.
192. Okay, I get it, please go on.
193. Please go on.
194. I can feel you.
195. I can understand that.
196. What other stuff relates to what you were telling me?
197. Could you keep talking about that?
198. I would like to hear more about that.
199. It doesn't sound like your done talking about it. Could you go on please?
200. I'm understanding you, but would like to hear more.
201. Talk more about when you are happy.
202. Help me understand more about how you accomplished that.
203. You said you felt bad about it—tell me more about feeling bad.

Client: It's like I am surrounded by darkness, everyone else is in the light, but somehow I must remain in the dark.

Therapist: I'm hearing what you are saying. Keep talking about this darkness. *or*

Therapist: Please continue.

Partial Transcript of Reflecting Pool Skills

Th = Therapist

Cl = Client

204. Th: Okay, so last week we talked about your desire to meet new people and not feel so nervous about being around others. We also talked about you getting yourself into social situations. (Summary)

Cl: Yeah, I wanted to tell you that I did go to see that woman I told you about.

205. Th: Uh, Okay. (Minimal Encourager)

Cl: Yeah, I felt a little funny just walking in and talking to her.

206. Th: You must have been a little nervous. (Empathy)

Cl: Yes, I was! My palms were soaked. I was really scared of what she might say.

207. Th: So you felt apprehensive about how it might go. (Reflection of Feeling)

Cl: Yeah. But it went okay, she was nice and . . . yeah, it went okay.

208. Th: So, I hear you saying your meeting went all right. (Paraphrase)

Cl: Well, I would have liked to have been a little smoother. You know what I mean. I think she could tell I was nervous.

209. Th: You believe that others should not be able to read your emotions, like when you are nervous. (Reflection of Meaning)

Cl: Well, I guess that's true. But, you know, women don't like guys who aren't sure of themselves.

210. Th: Tell me more about what women want in a man. (Prompts)

Cl: Well, they want you to be tough and rugged, strong, not show emotion or act like a baby at all.

211. Th: Not act like a baby. (Accent)

Cl: Well yeah. I mean, who wants to have to take care of someone.

212. Th: Okay, so what would that say about you if a woman had to take care of you? (Downward Arrow)

Cl: It would mean that I was weak.

213. **Th:** And being weak for a man means . . . (Downward Arrow)

Cl: It means that you are not a real man and that other people can take advantage of you.

214. **Th:** So, then what does it say about a man who allows others to take advantage of him? (Downward Arrow)

Cl: I guess, to me, it is like if you allow yourself to be taken advantage of, then after people use you, they will leave.

PRACTICE EXERCISES

Write your response, label the skill or skills used, then indicate your purpose for saying what you said.

Client: I am really feeling angry about the situation.

Response 1 _____

_____

_____

Client: It just made me nervous when she started talking about what would happen if we didn't turn in our homework on time.

Response 2 _____

_____

_____

Client: It probably sounds goofy to you, but I have no idea what I want to do for a living. I know, I'm forty-three years old, but I just don't know.

Response 3 _____

_____

_____

Client: Before the accident, I always thought that the worst thing was getting to work late. Now I have to worry about whether I will need more tests and surgeries. Life has really changed for me.

Response 4 _____

_____

_____

Client: Everyone thinks I need help with my drinking, but I don't think it's a problem. I just really enjoy having a few drinks with my friends.

Response 5 _____

_____

_____

CHAPTER 4

The Questioning Tree

The therapist uses questions to retrieve information, acquire insight, move to a deeper part of the client's story, or suggest that the client consider things in a different way. This technique is sometimes overused, especially by inexperienced therapists. Excessive questioning may also send the message to the client that his role is simply to answer such queries. Those significant cautions noted, however, questions still form a cornerstone for many theories of therapy. Questions may range from those that elicit short client responses to advanced inquires designed to prompt the client to assess or challenge some significant behavior.

Closed Question

Approach aligned with: Universal skill

Purpose: To have the client provide specific information. These questions usually promote brief client responses—one word or a short phrase. They are useful for retrieving pertinent, specific information and/or highlighting material the therapist believes the client should know or make use of in the moment, later in the session, or in subsequent sessions.

What the therapist does: The therapist asks the client a question that is intended to generate a short answer of one or a few words. Usually, these questions start with who, is, do, did, are, or does.

Examples:

215. Did anyone help you?
216. Do you get a break during the evening at all?
217. Are there times when you get a chance to sit down and relax?
218. How long does it take to finish all of your stuff?
219. Do your kids notice all the work you are doing?
220. Are you thinking about changing your schedule?
221. Are there days when you don't get everything done?
222. Do I understand that you do all of this alone?
223. Is there a way you can change your schedule at all?
224. Are things bad enough yet to change?
225. What percentage of your activities involve doing things for others?
226. Who treats you with the most respect and dignity?
227. Are you thinking about quitting?
228. Have you considered not doing so much for others?
229. Do you think anyone else working there is treated like you?
230. Who can give you a clearer job description?
231. Can you get along in your job as it is now?
232. Are you thinking you want a new position in the company?
233. Do you need my help in changing your role with the company?

Client: I guess I just never got a chance to learn how to handle stress in a good way.

Therapist: Of the people you know who handle stress wells who would you like to model yourself after?

or

Therapist: Among everyone you know, who handles stress the best?

or

Therapist: What one word best describes how you handle stress right now?

Open Question

Approach aligned with: Universal skill

Purpose: To promote a detailed discussion pertaining to a part of the client's story. The intent of these questions is to elicit lengthy responses from the client. In helping the client relate her story, further questioning on specific aspects of the client's life may be appropriate.

What the therapist does: The therapist asks a question that is intended to get the client to discuss an issue in greater detail (more than a few words). Open Questions usually start with how, why, or what.

Examples:

234. What is it like to be so busy?

235. How do you get all of that done?

236. What would happen if you refused to do the chores?

237. When the evening goes well, what is happening?

238. What is it like to have so many things waiting for you when you get home?

239. How might the family react if you suddenly stopped doing so much?

240. How would the family react to you if you refused to do the laundry?

241. Can you tell me what you feel after you finish all of your chores?

242. What have you tried to get the kids to help around the house?

243. What would have to happen for you to decide you have done your last chore?

244. What is it like for you when people notice what you do?

245. What options have you explored in relation to your problems at work?

246. How do others respond to you when you don't do their work?

247. What are some of the expectations placed on your coworkers?

248. What has been the worst experience you have had at work?

249. What has been the best experience you have had at work?

Client: Sometimes work is good, but most of the time I hate being there and really don't like the people I work with.

Therapist: When things are going well at work, what is happening?
or

Therapist: How do your coworkers relate to one another and to you while you're at work?

Checkout

Approach aligned with: Universal skill

Purpose: To insure that the therapist is hearing the client correctly. The technique can be linked to other skills such as confrontation, questions, or reflecting material back to the client; however, the key ingredient in this skill is making sure what has been sent by the client has been accurately received by the therapist.

What the therapist does: The therapist asks the client if what he has heard is correct or if the client is feeling that the therapist has understood him.

Examples:

250. Okay, let me see if I have this right . . .

251. Am I hearing you correctly that . . .

252. Did you say that . . .

253. Let me check something . . . did I hear that right?

254. So do I understand you right that . . .

255. You are saying that . . .

256. You said . . . am I hearing that right?

257. You said that you felt . . . am I hearing how you feel correctly?

258. You gave several examples there, they were . . . , did I catch all of them?

259. Do I have it correct that . . .

260. All right, is what you just said similar to . . .

261. Would I be correct to say to you that I heard you say . . .

262. Let me check out whether I caught what you were saying right, was it . . .

263. I want to make sure that I am hearing you correctly, you story is that . . .

264. In essence then, your feeling that . . . right?

265. Okay, so what you would like is to . . . did I get that correct?

266. Let me check something out with you, you feel that . . .

267. Okay, do I have it right that you want to be . . .

Client: So after I got done telling her about it, she just looked at me and walked away. I was hoping she would say at least something about it.

Therapist: So, if I understand it right, you wanted to hear her reaction to what you said?

Asking the Question

Approach aligned with: Individual Psychology

Purpose: To bring to the surface client goals and objectives, the price paid for the behavior, and the payoff for continuing the behavior.

What the therapist does: The therapist asks a question similar to the core question: "What would be different if you were well?"

Examples:

268. What would be different if you were well?
269. How will your life be different when the problem is no longer in your life?
270. What will be different when you are well?
271. What effect on your life will getting well have?
272. When you are better, what will be different?
273. What will change when you are better?
274. When things improve and you are well, what will be different?
275. How will improvements and your increased wellness change life?
276. As you improve, what will change in your life?
277. Now that you are on your way to being well, what will change in your life that you are most aware of?
278. What do you imagine will change when you are well?
279. When you are no longer depressed, how will your life change?
280. If things change for the better, how will your life be altered?
281. Thinking for a minute, and just hypothesizing, how do you see your life improving as a result of getting better?
282. What things will change in your life when you get to feeling better?
283. What would change if things were good in your life?
284. If things keep improving, and you get to feeling even better, things will obviously change. In what ways will your life be different?
285. Over time, as your life comes back to where you want it, things will change. What things are you most expecting to be different at that point?
286. You have been working really hard at improving things in your life, how do you see things changing as a result of your effort?

Cognitive Disputation

Approach aligned with: Cognitive-Behavioral therapy

Purpose: To help the client understand the faulty assumption on which the client is basing his belief and the subsequent thoughts and actions that occur as a result of that belief.

What the therapist does: The therapist asks the client to provide evidence or proof that the belief behind the maintenance of his fear/anger/hurt/embarrassment is actually logical or rational.

Examples:

287. What proof do you have that you are correct in assuming that no one at the party would like you to dance?

288. Does it make sense to you to believe that if you are embarrassed once at work, you will always be embarrassed at work?

289. Can you give me some evidence to support your notion that you are the worst student in the class?

290. You said that you feel as though the world is always watching you and waiting for you to make a mistake. I am curious, if this were an absolute truth, would it not be safer for you to hide in a cave away from others?

291. If you continue to believe that you were the reason your parents got a divorce, what effect will that have on the rest of your life?

292. Is it realistic to believe that you and your sister will never again talk or share anything important?

293. How can you show me that your belief about yourself is actually a fact and not just imagination?

294. What would someone else say in defense of your logic in regard to your statement that if you fail to pay one credit card on time you will always be in debt?

295. As you said, you are always the life of the party, and that sometimes gets you in trouble. I wonder what proof you have that you must always be the life of the party?

296. What effect will it have on the rest of your life if you continue to tell yourself that you always must be perfect?

Client: Having depression is the worst thing in the world. It is like having a scarlet letter "W" for worthless.

Therapist: What evidence do you have to support this idea that depression equals worthlessness?

Circular Questioning

Approach aligned with: Individual therapy and Family therapy

Purpose: To incorporate alternatives into the client's or family's story. The technique uses questions framed in a way that asks client(s) to think about the connections between and among family members. Rather than direct didactic questioning, this technique encourages the client to focus on the function of the problem within the entire system.

What the therapist does: The therapist asks a question rooted in surfacing the relationship others have with the issue.

Examples:

297. Who among everyone in your family has the clearest picture of the issue?

298. Who among everyone you know has the most hope for the family?

299. Among your immediate and distant family and all of your friends, which people have the least amount of hope for the relationship to succeed?

300. What does the person who knows the most about the situation know that the rest of the family doesn't?

301. Who sees how close the two of your really are?

302. Which of your children is most apt to pick up on your subtle language?

303. When things are really going well, who is most often promoting the happy times?

304. Which family member has the keenest eye for changes in the family?

305. How might someone from outside the system be making sense of the changes you have described?

306. Thinking back to when the problem started, who in the family was the first to notice how it was affecting the family?

Client: It's hard for us to even be in the same room. It's like mixing gasoline and fire, and it has been like that for as long as I can remember.

Therapist: Who is most affected by this combustible situation? *or*

Therapist: Besides you two, among everyone you know, who is the most affected by this volatile relationship?

Externalizing the Problem

Approach aligned with: Brief therapy

Purpose: To help the client see the problem as a separate entity from herself. It is used in family therapy to help the family focus less on who owns the problem and more on how to unite as a unit and resolve to defeat the problem.

What the therapist does: The therapist encourages the client to view the problem as outside of herself. This is done by statements and questions that focus on the effect of the problem as an entity unto itself. The therapist can also try to shed light on the amount of energy the problem has taken from the client or the way in which the problem tricked the client to join it.

Examples:

307. When you think of this depression thing—what color is it?

308. In terms of your relationship to being afraid of being in a large group of people, what name would you give it?

309. Now that you have named your sense of depression as the blob, I'm curious how it recruited you into being a willing partner?

310. As a family, what name would you give to this difficult morning routine you described?

311. What color is this thing that tricks you into believing you are not worthy of love?

312. Okay, now I want you to tell me what shape you see when you think about the pain of losing your job.

313. How did this lumpy, yellowish green thing convince you to do that against your better judgment?

314. Who among everyone you know has the best view of what the "ugly messy anger thing" does to get you to act out?

315. Okay, so now let's work together as a family can. Who will sound the alarm when they see that the morning gremlin has returned?

316. What smell do you associate with this "gloomy monster"?

317. How did the problem trick you into believing it was a friend?

318. In which instances did the problem convince you to do things that were against your better judgment?

319. How much of your time and energy has this problem talked you into spending on it?

Miracle Question

Approach aligned with: Brief therapy

Purpose: To have the client envision the world as if everything is okay. It also helps the therapist hear the core or critical issue for the client.

What the therapist does: The therapist asks the client how his life would be different or what he would notice to be different if the problem were to suddenly go away. This question is anchored in envisioning that a miracle has occurred.

Examples:

320. If you were to go to bed tonight and sometime during the night a miracle happened that caused your problem to disappear, what would be the first sign that things had changed when you woke up?

321. Let's say that tonight after you go to sleep, a miracle happens. You are not sure exactly how it happened but your problem suddenly goes away. When you wake up tomorrow, how will your life be different?

322. If a miracle happened after you went to bed tonight, what effect would that have on your problem?

323. How would your problem change if you went to bed tonight and while you slept a miracle happened?

324. What would change in your life if, say, during the night tonight, something happened and there was a miracle?

325. Now, I'm going to ask you something kind of strange . . . what if you were to go to sleep tonight, just as you normally do, and something different happened. A miracle took place while you slept. What would that miracle be?

326. If a miracle happened tonight and you woke up tomorrow and the problem was solved, outside of you, who would be the first to notice the change?

327. If a miracle happened tonight and you woke up tomorrow and the problem was solved, how would the world be different?

328. I know this is a goofy question . . . but if you were to suddenly realize that a miracle had taken place and the problem went away, what would be the change in your life?

Probe

Approach aligned with: Universal skill

Purpose: To bring to the surface specific information germane to the issue being discussed.

What the therapist does: The therapist asks the client about specific information. Questions usually start with who, what, when, or how. Questions are asked in a way that elicits one- or two-word responses. These questions are a form of Closed Question.

Examples:

329. Who among everyone you know has a good sense of what is happening?

330. Where were you when you heard that news?

331. What was the strongest emotion you had when you learned that you had been accepted into graduate school?

332. How many people do you know that have a similar set of beliefs as you?

333. What one word would you give to describe how your mother felt about you leaving home at that point in time?

334. Tell me who it was that provided the most hope for you when you were going through this before?

335. If you could connect the past and present versions of this dilemma in one or two words, what would they be?

336. Which of the resources you mentioned you have will be most important to you as you set off on a new career?

337. In thinking about your future, who do you think will be most important in making a strong case for you remaining in school?

338. What was the thing that first caught your eye as being a positive in her?

339. You mentioned wanting to understand her perspective better. Can you give me a word or two that defines where she is at with all of this?

340. When did you start to know that things were going to be all right in your life?

Client: As I thought about it, I wasn't sure whether or not to stay and try to figure it (the relationship) out.

Therapist: What signaled to you that it was worth it to stay in the relationship?

Forced Choice Question

Approach aligned with: Universal skill

Purpose: To have the client articulate direction or have the therapist embed positive reframes.

What the therapist does: The therapist asks a question that forces the client to choose between two or more options, choices, or alternatives.

Examples:

341. Who do you believe will be of the most help to you as you begin the process of healing?

342. As we have spent our time together, we have discussed a number of different issues. We have discussed anger management, decision making, communication skills, and awareness of nonverbal interactions. Which of these areas would you like to discuss as we proceed?

343. So as I hear you talking about the issue, I wonder which of these two things people notice most quickly about you. Is it your good intentions or your strong level of effort?

344. Was it that your mother was upset with your desire to be independent or your willfulness in expressing your opinion?

345. As you think about the things your parents did to you growing up, it seems you discuss their desire to keep you from your dreams. Was it that they wanted you to learn to work for what you wanted in life, or was it that they wanted to help you learn to overcome difficulties in a safe place?

346. There have been several things that you have talked about in relation to having depression. I want to take a minute and hypothesize about how this depression thing came into your life. Was it that it weaseled its way in when you weren't paying close attention, was it that somehow it tricked you into thinking it was a friend, or was it that it destroyed another part of your life that you had not been living to its fullest?

347. As we have talked about different career options, I want to hear about which is most important to you right now—working with people, working with ideas, or working with things?

348. When things get back to better for you, and the problem goes away, what will you notice first—more energy, feeling happier, or getting along with others better?

The Terrible Question

Approach aligned with: Universal skill

Purpose: To have the client consider that she will have to be diligent to prevent a relapse and/or to have the client make overt any hidden agenda or intentions (many times unknown to them) that might cause them to return to the previous state.

What the therapist does: The therapist asks the client a question that asks what would have to happen for the previous state to return. Variations of this skill may include questions that ask what the client or others might notice if the problem returns.

Examples:

349. Okay, I am going to ask you a terrible question. What would have to happen for the problem to return?

350. This is a terrible thought, I know, but what would you have to do to have the problem come back into your life?

351. We need to discuss for a few minutes the fact that sometimes problems return to us even when we do not expect them. What will be the first thing to alert you to the fact that the problem is back in your life?

352. I have a terrible thought here, but I want to have you talk about how you will defeat the problem when it starts to creep back into your life. What will you use to combat such a sneaky force?

353. As we know, problems may sometimes reinvent themselves and take on new forms as we go about our busy lives. This is a bad thought I have, but I suspect the problem you have just defeated will do its best to make things rough for you again. If I am right, you will need a plan to stop such an infestation. What things in your life will be most affected if this problem returns?

354. This is a terrible question. What would have to happen for you to have a problem similar to the one you had when you started therapy?

355. I have a terrible question here. But, I'm curious, you said that your wife noticed the changes you described in your affect and mood even before you did. What will she notice happening if the problem returns?

356. How will others around you become aware of the problem returning, that is, if it returns?

Triadic Questioning

Approach aligned with: Family therapy and Group therapy

Purpose: To bring to the surface new insight and meanings to discussions and connections between and among individuals.

What the therapist does: The therapist asks one member of the family or group how two other family members or group members relate and function together.

Examples:

357. Okay, Monique, I want to hear from you about the way your mom and dad talk to one another. What are you hearing them saying?

358. Now, let's take a minute and hear from someone who has been observing this interaction. Marg, what are you hearing Jim and Julio say to one another?

359. As we have been talking about how the family gets along, I want to know what you are seeing in the interaction between your brother and sister—how are they getting along?

360. I wonder what the other group members are seeing and hearing right now. Kenneth, can you describe how this interaction is going right now? What are you hearing them say to one another?

361. Okay, things are really getting heated. Bobby, you seemed to stay out of this mess. Be as detailed as you can be, what did you see happen?

362. If I understand the problem right, you are describing how when you wake up your son talks back to you, which causes you to get upset, and then the morning goes to hell rather quickly. So Kelly, you share a room with your brother—what do you see and hear happening between your mom and brother?

363. I wonder what the voice of an observer would provide us with. Billy, you have been watching this interaction all group. How are you seeing Anne and Meghan relate today?

364. As you reflect on the last week, keeping in mind that things are getting better in the household, what has changed in the relations between mom and dad? Let's start with Ahmad.

365. When you think about the last exchange we just saw between these two, who can share an observation of how they were getting along with one another?

Scaling Question

Approach aligned with: Brief therapy

Purpose: To identify the level or degree of intensity of the problem. These questions may also be used to discern changes in the magnitude of the problem.

What the therapist does: The therapist asks the client to put the problem, issue, or resolution on a scale, usually from one to ten. Then the therapist may explore actions the client could take to change his number.

Examples:

366. So we have been talking about how difficult this problem has been for you. It seems, as you said, that you have never felt this way. On a scale from one to ten—ten being the most—how much hope do you have for getting through this?

367. Obviously, as you just expressed, things are getting better. You must feel excited about that. On a scale from one to ten, how would you rate your sense of positive movement right now? Okay, then if you are a six right now, what would you have to do to go to a seven?

368. Last week you were a four on the scale, this week an eight. According to my math, that is a 100 percent gain in seven days. So in seven more days, at this pace you will be a 16 . . . correct?

369. I would like everyone in the family to take a turn and rate, on a scale from one to ten—one being poor, ten being excellent— your own level of effort in resolving this family issue.

370. As group members, let's each take a minute and quantify the level of trust we feel right now within this group. Let's use a scale from one to fifteen, with fifteen being absolute, complete trust. Where are you on that scale?

371. Before we get going, I wanted to have you self-assess your level of effort in finding a job. On a scale from one to ten—one being low, ten being high—where are you?

372. One of the things I am interested in finding out is your level of pain and discomfort regarding your last depressive episode. You said that when you realized it was upon you, you were really low. On a scale from one to ten—one being the lowest you have ever been in your life—how would you rate it? Okay, so on that same scale, where are you as you sit here today?

Collaborative Empiricism

Approach aligned with: Cognitive-Behavioral therapy

Purpose: To have the client consider whether what they are thinking is accurate and logical. This technique is used to help the client stop automatic thoughts that are illogical and/or based on false conclusions.

What the therapist does: The therapist asks the client to examine thoughts from a researcher's perspective. The client is taught to actually look for evidence regarding the particular thought in question.

Examples:

373. So what I heard you say was that everyone at work hates you. Let's see if we can find facts to support that. What evidence do you have to support that everyone hates you?

374. You mentioned that you were interested in asking him out but felt that you didn't look pretty enough. So I want you to ask at least seven people who would not lie to you about this question, whether or not this is true.

375. I heard you mention that you believe that your husband will never come around to understanding your position on this. I want you to go home tonight and make a list of at least ten things that have been really important to you that took some time for your husband to comprehend.

376. If it was true that you always make mistakes and get things wrong, shouldn't we be able to find all sorts of evidence of that in our therapy sessions? Can you help me see when you have done these things in here?

377. You seem to have some knowledge about the subject of friendship, right? And I heard you say that it is impossible for you to make new friends. I wonder what evidence you have to support that position.

378. When we talk about that issue . . . you seem to have a strong sense that nothing you ever do will have an effect on it. I am curious what support you have to offer in proving that this is true . . . that you have no effect on it.

379. You said that there is no way you could exercise three times this week. I want you to try an experiment. Exercise twice and then see what happens when you try to exercise the third time—see what gets in your way and makes you fail.

Communication Clarification

Approach aligned with: Group therapy

Purpose: To enable clients to hear one another better. This technique is intended to focus group members on interactions and exchanges between and among them.

What the therapist does: The therapist asks the people involved in the discussion to make sure that they are being heard and that the other person is hearing the message that they intended to send.

Examples:

380. Janie, what did you just hear Jimmy say?

381. Okay, so I'm wondering what the core message you are trying to send is.

382. I know that there is something useful in what you just said, but right now I, and perhaps the other group members, are a little unsure of what you mean.

383. Chrissy, you just got some strong feedback from Selina. What did you hear her say?

384. What are the other members of the group hearing in this conversation?

385. Liza, I want to make sure that you are being heard clearly. Who in the group got what you just said the clearest, and how would they phrase it?

386. What is the main purpose behind what you are saying?

387. Can you clarify that statement?

388. So Amy and Erika are having a deep discussion. What are you hearing them say to one another, Fran?

389. Can anyone clarify the message Linda is sending to Kristen?

390. What are you all hearing as the message from Sedona to Kay?

391. I hear you saying something that seems important, but I'm unsure the message is being received as you intend it. What is it that you want Fran to hear from you right now?

392. As we are all hearing this conversation, I am wondering what you all are hearing Mary say to Ray?

393. We just had an emotional interaction, I'm sure each of you had your own personal reactions to it. If you could take a minute to set that aside, tell the group what you heard being said by these two?

Partial Transcript of Questioning Tree Skills and Techniques

Note: Both this partial transcript and the full transcript in Chapter 13 show the use of questions. It is wise and warranted that therapists, especially those in training, understand that asking a lot of questions in a session is usually counterproductive. To this end, we suggest that *real sessions should have very few questions* as compared to the following fictional partial transcript. We have created our transcript to provide you with examples of the questions in context as opposed to suggesting that good therapy is similar to an interrogation or rapid-fire succession of questions directed at the client.

The following fictional transcript depicts a session with a couple.

Th = Therapist

394. **Th:** So, looking back over where we have traveled, (to Mike) we have discussed your desire to be stronger in sharing your feelings, and (to Sue) we have discussed your interest in sharing the household duties and responsibilities. (Summary) I want to know which of these two directions we would like to begin with? (Forced Choice Question)

   Sue: We spent a lot of time talking about me last week, I think it would be nice to focus on Mike this week.

395. **Th:** Okay, Mike, is that okay with you? (Closed Question)

   Mike: Yeah, I guess, I mean I think I am doing a lot better this week with it.

396. **Th:** Mike, can you describe for us how you were able to better share your feelings this week? (Open Question)

   Mike: I just talked about stuff that was bothering me when it came up, I didn't keep it in.

   Sue: I noticed that too, you shared with me that you didn't want my parents to come over Wednesday night. You wouldn't have done that before.

397. **Th:** Okay, so let me check something out here with you two. I hear both of you saying that Mike was really different this week and shared how he felt about your parents coming over. (Checkout)

   Mike: Yep.

398. Th: So, Mike, in thinking about Sue and the kids, who was the first to notice that you were different in this way? (Circular Questioning)

Mike: Definitely Sue. She pays very close attention to what I say and do around the house.

Sue: Are you saying I pay too much attention to you?

Mike: No, I just know that you're good at noticing things.

399. Th: Okay, so Sue, there was something in what Mike said that made you think it was not a compliment. What did you hear Mike say? (Communication Clarification)

Sue: I heard him say that I notice things, but I also know that he tells me a lot of times to mind my own business.

400. Th: So Sue, just now you heard him say to you that you should mind your own business more? (Probe)

Sue: Yes.

401. Th: Okay, so I wonder what evidence you have to support your idea? (Cognitive Disputation)

Sue: Well, I guess it is just what he has said before about me.

402. Th: Mike, could Sue be correct that you were telling her to mind her own business? (Closed Question)

Mike: No. I like that she pays attention to me.

403. Th: So Sue, having heard what Mike said, and thinking of this as if you were outside the issue and it wasn't about you . . . (Sue interrupts)

Sue: Okay, yeah I get it, I see what you're saying. I guess you (to Mike) weren't really yelling at me right then.

Mike: No, no, I wasn't.

404. Th: When we started therapy, you two told me that your main goal was to communicate better. You said that you were a three on a scale from one to ten—do you remember? Okay, on that same scale—ten being exceptional at communication—what number do you both put on the last part of that interaction? (Scaling Question)

Mike: Five.

Sue: Six.

405. **Th:** Okay, so what was different? (Open Question)

     Sue: You made us look at what we were both saying.

     Mike: Yeah.

406. **Th:** So, here is a terrible question. What would make you go back to communicating at the three level? (The Terrible Question)

     Mike: If we assume things.

     Sue: I agree, if we don't take the time to listen and check things out with one another.

PRACTICE EXERCISES

Write your response, label the skill or skills used, then indicate your purpose for saying what you said.

Client: My boyfriend and I have been talking about marriage. But I'm not sure that's what I want.

Response 1 _____

_____

_____

Client: Ever since I retired, I've found myself floating away from people. No one is around to talk to or share moments with. I really miss Richard . . . I really miss how we were.

Response 2 _____

_____

_____

Client: The principal wanted me to come see you. She said you would listen to me. I just wish that my friends would stop telling those lies about me.

Response 3 _____

_____

_____

Client: When I found out I was pregnant six months ago, I thought that I would love being a mom. But, now, I'm not sure that I will be any good at it. You know, my mom made a lot of mistakes with my brothers and me.

Response 4 _____

_____

_____

Client: I went to the gaming meeting like I said last week. And when I got there, the other kids didn't want to play with me. They said I was too rough and stuff like that.

Response 5 _____

_____

_____

CHAPTER 5

The Framework

A vital and sometimes overlooked skill in therapy involves setting parameters for the actual therapy process. Initially, the therapist will explain how therapy works so that the client can understand both his role and that of the therapist (and others in the group, if it is a group experience). Maintaining the framework may also involve such techniques as analyzing what is happening within the therapy, interrupting or redirecting discussion, terminating therapy, and the like.

Structuring

Approach aligned with: Universal skill

Purpose: To provide clear direction to the client about how therapy works, what will be discussed, and the therapeutic format. Structuring is critical in helping the client understand both the general process of therapy and the particular approach being taken by the present therapist.

What the therapist does: The therapist gives a statement, either directly or indirectly, that helps the client understand how the session and, in general, the therapy will work.

Examples:

407. So as we begin today, I want you to tell me about what worked well for you last week.

408. Can you provide for me three solid examples of positive aspects of recovery?

409. Let's try to give some time to talking about how the problem has convinced you to remain with it.

410. We have been talking about the issues in your family. Can you give me some examples of some useful stuff from your family system?

411. As we start today I want to take a few minutes and discuss what has been most pressing for you this week.

412. In terms of therapy, what I try to do is provide an environment for you to learn more about yourself, learn to deal with some of the things that trouble you, and help you continue to grow as an individual.

413. If I heard you right, you want me to give you some advice on that issue. A general rule in the therapy process is for the therapist to avoid giving advice to clients.

414. You said that in your previous group therapy the group focused on the problems of the other people. In this group, we will focus primarily on the interactions between individuals, not just on problems.

415. You said that your main goal in being here was to learn more about dealing with your anger. How does talking about your childhood connect to your increased anger-management skills?

416. We will meet for fifty minutes each week, for the next three weeks. At that time, we will decide what the best course of action will be for your continued growth and development.

Here and Now

Approach aligned with: Group therapy, Gestalt therapy

Purpose: To focus the group and individual members on the actions, behaviors, thoughts, and communication that is currently happening.

What the therapist does: The therapist makes a direct statement or asks a question of the client or group that focuses the attention on the present situation.

Examples:

417. Okay, so you said you felt bad yesterday. What impact does that have on how you feel or what you are doing in this group right now?

418. Now that we have told our stories for being in group, I wonder what is happening right now. Are we sizing each other up? Are we trying to figure out each other's deeper seated problems?

419. Okay, Fransisco, so you said that you have trouble asserting yourself. Who in the group do you think you will have the easiest time asserting yourself with?

420. You said your problem is controlling your temper. Right now, how are you doing controlling your temper?

421. You laughed when you said that you had just been out in left field for the last twenty minutes. What do I do that causes you to tune out like that?

422. If you were able to overcome your fear of rejection, what might you share with Mohammed about your feelings toward him?

423. We have a covert group norm of acting really nice toward one another, right? Okay, so who is the leader of that norm, who maintains it, and who is most opposed to it?

424. How are you displaying your dislike for this group right now?

425. Among the group members, whom do you trust the most right now to give you an honest opinion?

426. My reaction to this discussion is that of boredom. From my perspective it makes more sense that we talk about things happening here and now in this group.

427. Right now, there is something important happening in this group. As we discuss the trials and tribulations from our past, we are doing something really important in the moment. I would like to take some time right now to discuss what we are doing right here in the moment.

Process Illumination

Approach aligned with: Group therapy

Purpose: To discuss with and among the group members what has been happening in the group from a meta- or overall perspective over a certain time period (e.g., the last thirty minutes, the last two sessions, etc.).

What the therapist does: The therapist makes a statement or asks a question about how the group has been functioning, what has been happening, how decisions have been made, or other information that the group should discuss to overtly decide if they want to keep functioning in that way.

Examples:

428. What have we as a group been doing for the last thirty minutes?

429. It seems to me that we spent the first half of this session talking about things from the past. Does anyone else have that sense?

430. There has been a large volume of discussion about what the group norms should be. I'm curious about how we decided to spend so much time talking about our norms.

431. What does our group do when individuals talk about things that are extremely emotional to them?

432. How safe is it in this group for people to share their personal stories?

433. Some of the things that we have done this session have been to talk in general terms about issues, avoid confrontation, and tell group members that they should not worry about their issues.

434. As a group, we shift focus from member to member as soon as they show affect.

435. Throughout this session we have asked group members a lot of questions. We have been mining for something.

436. I am secure in the knowledge that we as a group would rather talk about things that are out there rather than those that are in here.

437. This week we really focused on material in the here and now. It appeared that our conversations were much deeper and fuller.

438. I am curious. What have you each observed as the main theme for our discussion this week?

Technical Expert

Approach aligned with: Group therapy

Purpose: To disseminate useful and meaningful information to the group participants about the role, function, expectations, or norms of the group.

What the therapist does: The therapist makes direct statements about the group that shares information necessary for operation of the group.

Examples:

439. This group will run for twelve weeks, meeting each Monday at 5:00.

440. In my experience as a group leader, I have noticed that groups run well when the norms are talked about and highlighted throughout the group process.

441. We need to allow people to finish their statements before jumping in and talking.

442. As the leader I can see that we need more clear direction for this group.

443. We need to do more sharing of feelings and thoughts for this group to work well.

444. The fact that some people share a lot and others share very little has stymied our group movement.

445. I need to interrupt your conversation right now. The two of you are talking about something outside the group. We need to bring our focus back to the matter at hand.

446. There are several stages to group. First we form the group, second we create some norms for the group, third we have a rather stormy period, fourth we work toward goals, and finally we adjourn the group.

447. In my groups, we usually spend some time sharing what brought us here to be in group therapy.

448. I think we need to be more active as a group in confronting behaviors that are not acceptable to our self-created norms.

449. Okay, as we come to a close this week, I want to remind you that we are meeting again for each and every week over the next two months.

450. Okay, we need to allow everyone to have a voice in this group. So let's remember that we need to take time and to listen to others and not talk over them.

Model-Setting Participant

Approach aligned with: Group therapy

Purpose: To demonstrate for clients how to share information, self-disclose, and give feedback to and receive feedback from others.

What the therapist does: The therapist, in a nondefensive way, shares his thoughts with the group regarding an issue in a direct statement.

Examples:

451. It must have been difficult for you to share that with the group.

452. I am feeling very close to you right now.

453. Right now, I am feeling I can share the most with Mary and Tom.

454. I am feeling a bit judged by the group right now.

455. I really like the fact that you were nervous about sharing that information—I too am nervous about sharing personal information—it really scares me.

456. When you mention that you have had trouble talking with strangers, I can relate, because I have a similar concern . . . like I am being judged by them and won't meet their expectations.

457. As you were talking, I had a strong reaction to what you said. I really felt a sense of closeness and warmth toward you.

458. I feel most connected to you as well.

459. I heard you say that I make statements sometimes that make little sense to you. I have heard that before and am aware that that is one of the things about me that I would like to change . . . you know, to be more clear and direct with people.

460. I really feel free to explore in this group. I feel and believe that it is related to some of the norms in this group, like openness, concern, confrontation, and emphasis on the here and now.

461. I feel sad about what you just shared.

462. It touches me to have you share such a personal experience.

463. As I heard you telling her that she was not thinking correctly, I began to feel very unsafe for both Mary and myself.

464. I am feeling like I have a place in this group. I feel like I am heard, respected, and, when not understood by others, asked to clarify my statement.

465. Right now, in this moment, I am experiencing both joy for our group and how far we have come, and sadness that we will be ending soon.

Blocking

Approach aligned with: Family therapy and Group therapy

Purpose: To stop unwanted or problematic discussions from centering around or on vulnerable group or family members. This technique can be either verbal or nonverbal. It is a skill that is used to remove a client from the hot seat when being on the hot seat is counter-productive to either the individual or group.

What the therapist does: The therapist uses either a verbal or non-verbal response intended to stop the discussion and refocus the attention onto either another subject or the process of what just occurred.

Examples:

466. Okay, so let's take a minute and discuss what has been happening here.

467. Lionel, I am sensing that you have heard a lot in the last few moments and may need some time to digest all of the new information.

468. Can we as a group decide that Mary has gotten enough feedback and that perhaps we need to move on to another topic?

469. This is a pretty emotional time right now in the group. Can we take a minute and explore how we got here?

470. Eddie, you have heard a lot from your family. I suspect that it may have been too much for you to make sense of in the moment, would it be helpful if we moved on?

471. Obviously there is a lot of emotion for you on this subject . . . but maybe Peggy has heard enough right now.

472. Okay, rather than staying on this line of discussion I want to see what you all think about another topic, such as . . .

473. Malcom, I can see that you are really having a lot of difficulty with all of the information coming your way. I should have stopped this discussion earlier. I am sorry. Would it help if we talked about something else for a few moments?

474. Devon, what would you like to have Elaine say in this moment to get you to stop talking to her about this subject?

475. What does the group need to hear to assure them that they have been heard by Meghan?

476. Wow, that was a lot of information for Donna to take in all at once. I suspect that she needs a few moments to gather her thoughts—let's give her some time to do just that. Kim, please continue talking about . . .

Changing Questions to Statements

Approach aligned with: Group therapy, Gestalt therapy

Purpose: To help clients change a question they have to a direct statement that starts with "I." Used frequently in group therapy, this technique promotes more direct communication and fewer indirect questions and statements.

What the therapist does: The therapist asks the client to take a question they asked or statement that is not anchored in "I" terminology and change it to a direct statement, usually starting with "I."

Examples: (*Note:* The first statement is the original client statement to a fellow group member; the second statement (in brackets) is what the therapist would help them create and say.)

477. Are you upset? [I believe that you are upset.]
478. Don't you think that you should talk to her? [I think you should talk to her.]
479. Is that what you really want? [I do not think that is what you really want.]
480. Do you think you might be happier without them? [I feel as though you would be happier without them.]
481. Are we going to have to talk about emotional stuff? [I am nervous about talking about emotional stuff.]
482. Is Brenda upset with us? [I feel as though you are upset with us.]
483. Do you think we would be better off apart? [I am thinking that we might be better off apart.]
484. Does that upset you? [I get the sense that that upsets you, or I am upset with that type of behavior by other people.]
485. Don't you feel bad about that? [I think you should feel bad about that.]
486. Are you happy with that choice? [I feel you should be happy with that choice.]
487. Why are you still with him? [I feel and believe that you would be better off if you were not with him.]
488. Did you pray on it? [I believe that you should turn to God for an answer to your question.]
489. You are not happy with that are you? [I feel that you should not be happy with what occurred.]
490. I just want to know, how you can stay so calm about what he did to you? [I believe you should be upset with him and show it.]

Capping

Approach aligned with: Universal skill

Purpose: To help the client move away from emotion-laden discussions and into more cognitive-based dialogue. This technique is used a lot when terminating the therapy relationship. It is also used to help the client move away from overly emotive responses.

What the therapist does: The therapist asks a question or makes a statement that is likely to elicit a cognitive or thinking response as opposed to an emotional or affective response.

Examples:

491. So you felt really bad about what you did. What were you thinking in that moment?

492. Now that you have had some time to express your feelings on the issue, I'm wondering what you think your brother was thinking?

493. So you were happy, exhilarated, and energized. Along with this you were thinking . . .

494. Your emotional response was sadness and regret. What thoughts go along with such feelings?

495. I hear you expressing a lot of feelings. I am wondering what was happening in your mind . . . what your thoughts were at that time?

496. What if someone outside your family witnesses the same action . . . a passive observer with no emotional attachment to the scenes. What would they be thinking?

497. As we get to the end of our time, I am wondering how your thoughts have changed as a part of this therapy?

498. You mentioned that you were very happy about our time together and that some things had changed. I want to hear about the things that have changed in regard to your beliefs or thoughts on the subject of alcoholism.

499. It sounds like that really touched your heart. I am wondering what, if anything, from that changed your thinking?

500. Okay, so as we continue here, I want to hear you talk a little more about your pain, but I want you to think about what others see when your are showing your pain.

501. Give me a couple of words that symbolize the emotion you are showing right now.

Clarifying the Purpose

Approach aligned with: Group therapy

Purpose: To help the group members remember or rehear the purpose of group therapy. It helps focus the discussion and bring the group back to the core issue(s) in therapy. It can also be used effectively in family therapy to help refocus the system on the issue at hand.

What the therapist does: The therapist asks a question or makes a statement that encourages group members to look at the meta-perspective of what they are doing, what the global or core issue to be explored is, and how they are meeting their objective.

Examples:

502. Okay, so now, to bring us back to the reason we are here—what does this discussion have to do with drugs and alcohol?

503. We need to remember that we are in this group because we have difficulty asserting ourselves. How has that lack of assertiveness reared its head in the last few minutes?

504. Remember, this group is about dealing with grief and loss.

505. We need to focus on the group norm of not interrupting one another. As a group we have not done well with that this week.

506. So how does the discussion we have had in the last half hour pertain to the topic of anger management?

507. This is a group that focuses on the connections we make with others and the way that we are viewed by others.

508. Remember that the purpose of this group is to help you gain insight into your compulsions.

509. What we are doing this week is trying to focus on how others see our behaviors in the group.

510. The reason we are meeting like this is to work through your feelings of abandonment.

511. How does that relate to the intention of this group?

512. This group is about how to relate to others. I am curious as to how we have been moving toward acquiring insight into such actions.

513. As we have talked over the last few minutes, I have been wondering what it is that we are talking about in relation to our overall group goal.

Defining the Problem/Issue

Approach aligned with: Universal skill

Purpose: To help the client recognize or clarify the presenting problem or issue. It helps direct the therapist and client into discussions about the problem and how to manage or deal with it.

What the therapist does: The therapist highlights with the client what it is that the client wants help with through therapy. Throughout the therapy process, the client and therapist should reexamine the problem or issue as it may change or morph into something new.

Examples:

514. So the problem is isolation?

515. You said that your main goal for therapy was to connect better with others, right?

516. The overarching dilemma you have is about how to handle it when people ask you to do things for them.

517. You need help with your anger?

518. You have come to therapy to help you get along better with your spouse.

519. Of all of those things, the most pressing issue in your life today is . . . ?

520. You mentioned a lot right there, can you help me out here . . . what is the most important thing for you to get help with of all of those you listed?

521. Your life would be better if you had a stronger sense of intimacy.

522. You need help finding a career path.

523. It sounds like your major goal is to get better grades.

524. So as you have explained things to me, you have expressed that you want more freedom, more independence, and to have your parents get off your back. Is it safe to say that the issue is that you want to be more autonomous?

525. So the core issue is confusion.

526. What I hear you saying is that you want to be accepted by others.

527. If we described the major issue in your life right now, could it be that we are describing a lack of enthusiasm on your part?

Defining Goals/Objectives/Outcomes

Approach aligned with: Universal skill

Purpose: To highlight what the client wants out of therapy.

What the therapist does: The therapist usually states in a clear question, comment, or statement what she thinks the client would like, or asks them what they want.

Examples:

528. So your goal this session is . . .

529. You will have to accomplish some things in order to meet that goal. What two or three things do you want to get a better handle on that will help you be more independent?

530. What would you like out of therapy?

531. If things work out well for you in therapy, what will be different?

532. How will these sessions have a positive impact on your life?

533. When we get done with our time together, what do you expect to be different for you?

534. I hear your main goal or objective to be controlling your emotions.

535. Am I to understand that you want to have a more open and friendly relationship with your mother?

536. You've had therapy before. What would you like out of our time together?

537. Tell me about what you think this therapy will do for you.

538. So I hear your goal as being to better understand both yourself and the way the world around you works.

539. I am hearing you say that your goal is to have a stronger image of who you are.

540. You said that you had really thought a lot about your goals for therapy. Do I have it right that your main objective is to . . .

541. You said that you have been in therapy before. I am interested to know what your goal is for our work together.

542. What is your goal for therapy?

543. What do you want to get out of therapy?

544. If our work together is useful to you, what will be different for you when it is complete?

545. When we decide that our work together is complete, and your life is much better, what will be our signal?

546. What will tell you that you no longer need a therapist?

PRACTICE EXERCISES

Write your response, label the skill or skills used, then indicate your purpose for saying what you said.

Client: I'm just so sad about it. Like no one else cares how much this hurts me and I just feel so bad for her and everything. I must sound really stupid, but it's just how I feel about it.

Response 1 _____

_____

_____

Client: It seems like all I do is get up, go to work, come home, and watch TV. I guess that on the weekends, I have some time to reflect on the situation, but I usually just try to get either caught up or ahead on work for the next week.

Response 2 _____

_____

_____

Client: Well, yeah, I guess that's right, I mean, sometimes it is hard for me to get up and going in the morning. I guess it started a few years ago, but anyhow, I just sometimes want to lay around and think about how things used to be.

Response 3 _____

_____

_____

CHAPTER 6

....

Looking for Clear Skies

Much of the therapy effort involves an attempt to help the client move from a crisis or strong personal issue confronting her to a more positive state of mind. Care must, of course, be taken not to gloss over the client's pain too quickly. Using skills found in this section allows the therapist to offer pragmatic and specific ways to start the process of solution building.

Reframe

Approach aligned with: Brief therapy

Purpose: To take the deeper meaning of what the client is saying and frame it in a more positive way. Reframes are used to provide the client with a new meaning to an old story. Reframes must not be too extreme in changing the deeper meaning to the client or the client will reject the new frame. Using this skill, the therapist needs to (1) reflect deep meaning and (2) provide new information for the client.

What the therapist does: The therapist takes the essence of the statement made by the client and moves it from a negative frame to a more positive and hopeful one.

Examples:

547. A lot of people depend on you.
548. You are dependable.
549. Somewhere you learned the value of a hard day's work.
550. You are the main cog in the family wheel.
551. No one takes the time to notice how much you do.
552. Your tasks are more than just a checklist, they are critical for the success of your children and family.
553. You give a lot to people.
554. It sounds like you are really dependable.
555. You are someone to be counted on.
556. You give to a lot of different people.
557. You are one of those people who does a lot for others without asking for much in return.
558. You have hope that things can be different.
559. You know there is another way to be helpful to others.
560. You have tried different ways to be productive at work.
561. For you, meaning from work is not just deadlines and production, it's the connection with the people you work with.
562. At work, you get a chance to see the good and bad in people.

Client: I feel like when I am at work, everyone there looks at me like I'm supposed to do things for them.

Therapist: Your coworkers see you as generous. *or*

Therapist: I hear you saying that your coworkers feel they can depend on you.

Exploring Alternatives

Approach aligned with: Universal skill

Purpose: To help the client look at other possibilities in her story. The therapist promotes thoughts, awareness, and new insights into existing issues or concerns by encouraging the client to explore alternatives. In other words, what are the competing story lines available to the client?

What the therapist does: The therapist asks the client to reflect on possible alternatives to the existing presentation of the issue.

Examples:

563. What other possibilities do you see in regard to this issue?
564. Are there any other ways that you could accomplish that?
565. Give me at least three alternative explanations to your theory about your family.
566. Can that be explained in any other ways?
567. If you had to come up with another way of explaining the world, how would that be different?
568. Is there another version of this story . . . and what is it?
569. Who might see a different scenario . . . and what would they see?
570. You mentioned that your grandmother was able to overcome this same problem—how did she do that?
571. Are there any other explanations for what happened?
572. Could you do any other things in the future in regard to this issue?
573. What has worked in relation to finding a solution?
574. How might someone else in your family explain this?
575. You said that you felt as if everyone at work was upset with you. Can you think of a time when there was at least one person who was not upset with you at work?
576. How did you do things when you were feeling well?

Client: The way I see it is that if my parents hadn't gotten divorced when I was so young, I wouldn't have so much trouble with relationships.

Therapist: Do you have an alternative explanation for that?

Identifying/Building Strengths

Approach aligned with: Universal skill

Purpose: To highlight the strengths and assets the client has. By encouraging the client to think about things from his past that worked well, the client is provided a template for future behavior.

What the therapist does: The therapist makes a statement or asks a question designed to bring to the surface unrecognized strengths or assets.

Examples:

577. So one of the things you have going for you is a strong desire to help others.

578. You said that several years ago you overcame a similar issue. How did you do that?

579. It sounds like you are task-oriented, strong-willed, and hard-working.

580. When you were young, you feared nothing, right?

581. One of the strengths you believe you have is perseverance.

582. Being outgoing has served you well throughout life.

583. It appears that you listen well to the stories and problems of others.

584. Do you consider controlling your temper in heated moments an asset?

585. I'm curious which of the things you just talked about is most helpful to you in your daily life.

586. Taking things as they come is an important skill in your life. It has helped you handle tough situations with class and style.

587. It sounds as though you really work hard to get what you want.

588. You seem to have a strong sense of who you are.

589. Who, among all of the people you know, is most aware of your strong desire to care for others and be helpful to those in need?

590. As you think about the experiences you have had with others, what stands out to you as a strength?

591. So one positive you have is that you can get things done on time.

592. It sounds as if you see yourself as being an excellent employee who thinks about the greater good of the company you work for.

Linking

Approach aligned with: Group therapy

Purpose: To connect individuals within a group on a certain topic to promote greater discussion among the group members and increased cohesion between members.

What the therapist does: The therapist picks out situations in group when two people seem to be aligned on a topic and then makes such things overt for the group to observe.

Examples:

593. It sounds to me like you are describing a situation similar to the one Emmett described. Do I have that right, Emmett?

594. So now we have three examples of people in this group who are afraid of what the group will say when they disclose personal issues, is that right, Bobby, Paula Rae, and Kay?

595. Okay, so, Monique, was there anything in what Johnny said that connected with you?

596. That was a very clear example of dealing with loss. Who connected with the story, or has a similar sense of loss?

597. Karlem, you said a lot there, but what I caught was your reliance on others for direction. To me that sounds similar to what Petey was saying earlier.

598. So both Nancy and Marcia Jean have a similar issue they are dealing with. Who else can relate?

599. I heard several of you talk about the desire to be seen more clearly by others. Did I hear you all right?

600. Your statement about what this group will be doing tonight is interesting. Who else has similar questions in your head?

601. Who among the group would like to see more focus on feelings than thoughts?

602. Tanya's comment about feeling stronger as a result of this group is interesting. Who else is having a similar reaction?

603. I am feeling a connection to what you just said. Who else can link with the comment Henry just made?

604. It seems as though several of you are having a nonverbal reaction to what Maya just said. Who can align with her statement?

605. How many of you can really hear what Isidore just expressed?

606. Kermit, in what ways can you connect with what Grace just said?

Compliment

Approach aligned with: Brief therapy

Purpose: To encourage the family to keep working on defeating the problem. Using this technique, the therapist writes a message at the end of the session that is designed to be ego-aligned with the entire family. This part of the overall message attempts to get the family to agree with the therapist. It is a reframe or positive connotation of the effort the family has made toward working on the problem.

What the therapist does: The therapist takes a few minutes to develop, either by himself or with a team, a message that is intended to connect to the family as a way of getting them all to be supportive of the therapy.

Examples:

607. As a family you have persisted when other families might have crumbled.

608. It seems as though you as a family have a tremendous strength in being able to laugh about situations that might cause others to cry.

609. One of the most positive aspects of working with you is that we are reminded how powerfully strong a family system can be.

610. Your family has made it through the rough part of life. Now you are working together on focusing on and improving your current relationships.

611. Among all the families we have seen, you seem to have the most lighthearted approach to life.

612. We have learned a lot from you. One such thing is that some families can keep going even in the face of very difficult times.

613. You should feel very proud of this first step you have made toward family wellness.

614. Although each of you presents us with positive aspects to work with, we are struck by how cohesive you are with one another.

615. In spite of our best efforts to see you as individuals, as a family you have developed a bond that looks impenetrable to others.

616. As a team we find your desire to tackle such a difficult and pressing issue a signal of your overall wellness as a group.

Exploration

Approach aligned with: Universal skill

Purpose: To help the client discover new insights or new skills in dealing with current or past life problems. It is used predominantly to connect resources and client material with the goals of therapy.

What the therapist does: The therapist, either through a question or direct statement, asks the client to investigate alternative resources, meanings, or allies in relation to the problem.

Examples:

617. Let's take some time and focus on the skills you have that relate to getting away from your depression.

618. You mentioned that you have dealt with this problem in the past. How did you do that?

619. In what ways have you been successful when people press you to talk in a group setting?

620. Who among everyone you know will be your best ally in coping with the new pressure?

621. Having been away from your family for the last few weeks, what new insights or information do you have regarding how the system works?

622. If you were to change your response to that type of person, what from your set of tools and skills will be of the most help?

623. You mentioned that both you and your husband are trying hard to make the marriage work. I am curious what he brings to this process that is helpful?

624. What attributes have you noticed in yourself that seem to help you deal with loss and grief?

625. This is not the first time in your life that you have had to deal with such strong disappointment. How have you successfully handled such moments in the past?

626. What skills can you bring to dealing with this issue?

627. As a family, how have you been able to overcome and defeat the life problems that have occurred before?

628. It seems apparent to me that we all have to deal with problems in our lives. What resources have you been able to call on in the past to help you in such a task?

Focus on Exceptions

Approach aligned with: Brief therapy

Purpose: To focus the attention of the session on exceptions to the problem rules that the client believes are set in stone.

What the therapist does: The therapist makes overt those messages in the client's story that are different than the rules of the problem. This is done by either listening closely for exception stories or by asking the client directly for exceptions.

Examples:

629. It is amazing to me how strongly you feel about getting in trouble in school. You said that you are always in trouble in school. But, I have noticed that in our time together, you have not done anything to get into trouble.

630. I heard you strongly suggest the anger you feel toward your mom right now. I am struck by how you were able to hold that anger off when you two went shopping. Somehow you succeeded in doing this.

631. As you were talking about how difficult it is at home right now, I think it must be very powerful for you to see that, as evidenced by your story about having fun watching TV together, your family can get along.

632. From what you have told me today things are very difficult in your life right now. Somehow, however, you have been able to muster the strength to keep going in the face of such adversity.

633. I am a bit confused . . . you have talked for several sessions about how bad things are right now, you have made a strong case in this direction. Just then, however, you said that you had hope for things getting better . . . somehow you've decided things can be different.

634. You have been talking about how your parents don't seem to trust you . . . how they are always asking you what you are doing, who you are talking to. But then I heard you say when you go anywhere with your friend Emma, they don't do that at all. I get the sense you have noticed a difference in the relationship you have with her as opposed to others.

Interpretation

Approach aligned with: Universal skill

Purpose: To help clients rewrite or re-author their old stories by giving new meaning to experiences, actions, or beliefs about self, others, or the way the world works.

What the therapist does: The therapist takes past behaviors or current stories or thinking conveyed by the client and offers new explanations or theories for why they occurred in that way. Interpretations are similar to Reframes but do not always hold or have as a part of them a positive connotation.

Examples:

635. Could it be that your mother was actually trying to care for you and provide you with a chance to grow when she did that?

636. Have you considered that maybe his strong parenting style is an attempt to avoid making the same mistakes his father made with him?

637. Is it possible that there are times when you act out in anger to defend yourself against others?

638. Maybe, and I am just hypothesizing right now, but maybe you keep leaving good men because you don't believe you are good enough for them.

639. Is it possible that in her own mind Aretha thinks she is looking out for you by being so bossy?

640. Did you ever consider that you have developed this ability to cut people off emotionally in order to save yourself from being hurt?

641. One explanation could be that he acts like a child in order to get you to play in the role of parent. He feels good when he is being parented and pampered.

642. You said that you like the attention you get when you get into trouble. Could it be that you feel like you matter the most when you are in trouble?

643. Am I way off here when I say that perhaps the reason you feel that way is because of the way you were reared?

644. It is clear to me that you have been thinking about this without acting on it for too long. I think you may be afraid that if you change too much your husband will not be able to keep up or will stop loving you.

Metaphor

Approach aligned with: Universal skill

Purpose: To provide the client with a story or simple statement that compares two dissimilar objects—the client's thoughts or behaviors and a more palatable object. The goal of this skill is to make the client more aware of his behavior and its effect on himself and others. The therapist can also prescribe metaphorical tasks to alleviate the presenting problem.

What the therapist does: The therapist provides the client with a phrase, story, or fable that connects indirectly to what is being discussed in therapy. Care must be taken on the part of the therapist to either make the connection overt to the client or keep the metaphor separate enough from the client so as to work covertly.

Examples:

645. It seems as though you have a desire to be the glue that holds this family together.
646. You are like the mighty oak holding itself strong against the powerful wind.
647. It sounds as though you are the family thermometer.
648. You really want to be the foundation upon which the family is built.
649. I get the impression you like to be a cog in the wheel.
650. Sasha, I think you do a wonderful job of voicing the concern of your family members to one another. For the next few minutes, I want you to go around and stand behind each family member and give voice to their main concerns. They are to each move their mouth as if they were actually doing the talking.
651. As a family, you have worked hard at forming strong relationships among one another. In this, however, some of the roles have become more than you would like. I want you to cook dinner together, but I want mom to take direction from Lynn, Lynn to take direction from little Nicholas, and dad to give direction to little Nicholas. I suspect this dinner will be a great success.
652. It sounds like you are the black hole for the emotions presented to you by your family.
653. When times get difficult, you run like the Mississippi River.
654. Do I have this right, you are like a giant boulder, impervious to any of the forces of nature?

Redefining

Approach aligned with: Universal skill

Purpose: To decrease client reactance to the therapist and the problem by providing a new meaning for the problematic behaviors. This skill is similar to Reframe.

What the therapist does: The therapist offers a positive connotation for the problematic behaviors or actions described by the client.

Examples:

655. Okay, so if I hear you right, you are talking about how your son's misbehavior makes the two of you focus hard on how to work together on parenting him. So, in essence, he is helping to maintain your strong bond with one another.

656. So when you become extremely emotional around your family you see that as a bad thing, but, perhaps you should consider that you are acting as the voice of the family, the emotional part, that is.

657. Am I correct in understanding that your apprehension of being intimate with him, although troubling, could also be a way of saying you are not ready for this type of commitment?

658. Does it make sense that maybe your talk about your family's fighting and bickering about the small stuff is a sign of real strength and caring for one another and your desire not to let small stuff get too big?

659. Is there a part of you that agrees with the notion that in some ways, the lessons you have learned your first two years of college, although painful and difficult at times, are blessings in helping you achieve your future dreams and aspirations, especially completing college in the next few years?

660. Can you see how an outsider may view the problem of being nonassertive as also a sign of being respectful to others?

661. So as a family, you have tried a lot to change this behavior, especially the part about trusting one another more fully. To me, the issue appears to be both trust in one another and, to a greater degree, trust in oneself.

662. So the pain of your childhood could also be considered in terms of the time of life when you developed a sense of being stronger.

PRACTICE EXERCISES

Write your response, label the skill or skills used, then indicate your purpose for saying what you said.

Client: I just don't know what to do to make him behave. Every time we go out in public, like to the store, he acts like the worst kid in the world.

Response 1 _____

_____

_____

Client: I think we have a good relationship, but at times she doesn't listen or show me any respect.

Response 2 _____

_____

_____

Client: When they told me I had AIDS I wanted to die right then and there. But over time I have learned to live with it. I guess my main mission in life right now is to help little kids with AIDS.

Response 3 _____

_____

_____

Client: After the war, I came home and expected things to be back to normal. You know, they don't talk to you about how to deal with life again. I just can't get those images out of my mind.

Response 4 _____

_____

_____

Client: I keep asking myself why my life has to be so much harder for me than for other people.

Response 5 _____

_____

_____

CHAPTER 7

....

Chasing Down Mirages

A mirage is simply a manifestation of how a person wants things to be instead of how they really are. In dealing with the client's distorted view of reality, the therapist uses a set of skills designed to dispute the client's story. Care must be exercised here because while such efforts are incredibly valuable to the client when they are delivered well, they can be counterproductive when they are done incorrectly.

Confrontation

Approach aligned with: Universal skill

Purpose: To provide the client with information about inconsistencies, incongruities, or mixed messages sent by the client. The therapist may make use of client's expressed thoughts, feelings, emotions, or actions in providing such feedback.

What the therapist does: The therapist makes a statement that draws attention to discrepancies in the client's words, actions, or story. This statement may be direct and straightforward or indirect and subtle.

Examples:

663. Earlier this session you said that you felt happy that your mother left, now you have just said that it upsets you to think of her gone. Can you clarify these two statements for me?

664. As you say that you're not happy about that, I notice that your face seems to have a smile on it.

665. You said that your dad was hard on you as a child and that you didn't want to be the same way to your kids, so I am unsure what you mean when you say you have to be tougher on your kids than anyone else.

666. You have been telling us that you want help with this issue and that you are willing to try anything to make it go away, yet you did not do the homework assignment from last week.

667. If you are unable to do anything right, how is it that you got to this appointment on time, well dressed, and ready to work on things?

668. You just said that things are going well for you at school yet your mom here says that you are failing every class. Are we all defining "well" in different ways?

669. You say that that doesn't bother you, but as I am sitting here watching you I notice you shifting a lot in your seat.

670. As you say that you are pleased with the outcome your voice seemed to drop, and you looked at your feet, and you began to wring your fingers.

671. You said that no one helps keep the house clean, and yet I just heard you say that your oldest daughter cleans her room once a week.

Observation

Approach aligned with: Group therapy

Purpose: To make an action, thought, or behavior overt for the individual and the rest of the group to see. It is a form of confrontation.

What the therapist does: The therapist makes a direct statement that highlights something for the individual and/or group to focus on in relation to a behavior or action that has just occurred.

Examples:

672. Each time you respond to a comment made in this group, you answer "yeah, but."

673. I noticed that when you were talking about getting angry, there were a number of group members who dropped their heads and would not look at you.

674. As you were saying that you don't really care about what others think of you, I noticed you kept looking at Isidore.

675. When I heard you say that it seemed as though several other group members crossed their arms and sat back.

676. Every time someone in this group is confronted, it seems as though you jump in and try to minimize what the other group member is saying.

677. As I have watched you receive feedback, it seems as though you take a lot of time in developing a clear and articulate response to what has been said.

678. I was watching the other group members as you talked about losing your mother. Each member seemed to show, in a different way, that they had a reaction to what you said. For example, I saw one member begin to cry.

679. It seems as though what you are saying is an attempt to shut down the other members of the group.

680. I have observed that you are willing to put yourself out there for the group to inspect closely when other members would rather sit back and not be judged.

681. I have observed myself as being most critical to those who are critical of me first.

682. Has anyone else observed that when Sharita and Gamal talk about something they always turn to face each other?

Confirmation

Approach aligned with: Cognitive-Behavioral therapy

Purpose: To point out and alert the client to the fact that a previously modified behavior has returned.

What the therapist does: The therapist alerts the client that the unwanted behavior has returned. It is important that the client be prepared for such feedback.

Examples:

683. Are you aware that you are blaming others for your difficulties?

684. I see you have decided to get angry about something over which you have no control.

685. I noticed that you are avoiding eye contact again.

686. We talked about what you would need when your problematic behavior returned. I think I am seeing you do it right now.

687. In the last few minutes you have reverted back to acting like a child.

688. You seem to be parentifying me in this moment.

689. When you talk to me like that, I get the sense that you are placing me back into the role of child.

690. It seems as though you would like to go back to the relationship we had before of me being the child and you the adult.

691. So, for the last few minutes we have been talking as if you were the parent and I were the child.

692. I am unsure what to do with this, but you have gone back to acting out your childhood anger toward your mother with me.

693. I notice that you are no longer looking me in the eye.

694. One of the things that we have been working on in therapy has been your assertiveness. I noticed that you just let me roll over your original thought.

695. Correct me if I'm wrong, but did I just notice you feeling bad for yourself and engaging in self-pity?

696. As we continue our work together, let's go back and re-address your goal of clarifying what you mean to others without getting upset. Did you just get upset with me when I asked you to explain what you meant?

697. You're shaking your finger at me when you speak again.

Cutting Off

Approach aligned with: Universal skill

Purpose: To stop a client from rambling on about a subject or topic that is not germane to the discussion. Care must be taken not to offend the client or stop a train of discussion that may actually lead to something valuable to the client. In other words, the therapist must weigh the pros and cons (respecting the client's right to talk vs. helping focus the client back on the topic or issue).

What the therapist does: The therapist uses verbal and/or nonverbal skills to either slow down or stop the client and her current discussion.

Examples:

698. You have given me a lot here, let's slow down and refocus.

699. How does all of what you are saying relate to depression?

700. Okay, okay, give me a minute to digest all of that information.

701. I am sure that what you are saying connects for you, but I am not sure how it does. Can you help me?

702. What stands out from everything that you have just said in relation to issues in your marriage?

703. Hold it, now I'm a bit confused. What does all of this have to do with the problem you came in here with?

704. Wow, you really got rolling there. I am sitting here wondering what to do to get us back on topic. Any ideas?

705. You mentioned when we started today that you were really upset about how your mom treated you last week. How does all of this connect for you?

706. I am assuming that the deeper meaning to what you are talking about reflects a core component of the main concern, but I am having trouble making the connection.

707. Can you slow down and take a minute to reflect on what has just transpired?

708. Okay, you just said things that went in several directions. Can you pick out one thing for us to focus on in this session?

709. I'm going to stop us right here and start to summarize what we have covered this week.

710. Wow, that is a lot of information. I want to go back and have you talk about the day you realized it was time to move on.

Spitting in the Client's Soup

Approach aligned with: Individual psychology

Purpose: To remove the payoff of the behavior; to make the behavior less tasteful or rewarding.

What the therapist does: The therapist makes overt or identifies for the client the payoff of the behavior.

Examples:

711. Okay, so if I understand the behavior you are describing, it sounds like when your daughter comes home with a good grade you tell her that she is capable of doing more and that she then in turn looks to you for comfort and you two spend a lot of time consoling one another about the fact that she didn't receive the highest grade.

712. So when your wife agrees to have sex, you tell her that it is too late and that maybe the next day you would be less tired . . . and then she feels really bad.

713. So if I understand it right, Ian, you know that when you hit your sister it will really make your mom and dad mad at you, and then they work together in punishing you.

714. So the payoff you receive for acting out in school is to get attention from your grandfather, the one who really cares for you, right?

715. All right then, let me give back to you some of what I just heard to see if I understand it. You always have to top your husband's story at dinner parties so that other people will see you as superior to him. Is that right?

716. I'm unsure if this makes sense. You just said that the reason you do that is to get him angry so that he shows love to you. Did I get that right?

717. And how often do you bring up the fact that she was unfaithful to you? Each time you did it she showed a lot of remorse and guilt, right? When will that be enough?

718. I hear you saying that it feels good to put other people down so that you look good in front of others.

719. I'm not sure if this makes sense, but I get the sense that part of the payoff for doing that is to feel stronger than those around you. Is that accurate?

PRACTICE EXERCISES

Write your response, label the skill or skills used, then indicate your purpose for saying what you said.

Client: I try to sit still in class but fifty minutes is a long time. Sometimes I just need to get up and move around.

Response 1 _____

_____

_____

Client: Except for the fight we had last week, things have been better at home. The kids have been doing their chores, and Mary and I have been getting along really well.

Response 2 _____

_____

_____

Client: She is beautiful, smart, and really funny. I just wish that I had the guts to go and talk with her. I just get so nervous around her.

Response 3 _____

_____

_____

Client: The thing is, I think Mrs. Jones hates Native Americans. She treats us like we are always wrong.

Response 4 _____

_____

_____

Client: Yeah, this was my third DUI. So they said I needed therapy. So I guess we are supposed to talk about my drinking. But really it's just been bad luck that I have had those DUIs. The first one was after a wedding, the second one happened when I had a couple of drinks at dinner with my husband, and this last one was after a night out with my girls.

Response 5 _____

_____

_____

CHAPTER 8

···

The Supply Line

Third graders need third-grade school supplies. The army needs Humvees. Even monks living in the mountains of Tibet need certain supplies to maintain their way of life. Similarly, the therapy process, at times, necessitates that the therapist supply feedback and information to the client. Done effectively, the data may provide valuable insight to the client. However, when done poorly, clients may often react in one of two ways: the client thinks (1) the therapist is here to answer my questions, or (2) the therapist doesn't really get what is going on with me right now.

Affirmation

Approach aligned with: Universal skill

Purpose: To encourage further self-determination and personal insight.

What the therapist does: The therapist amplifies the attempt the client is making at understanding his own particular view of the situation. The therapist uses this skill to highlight strengths and positive insight by the client.

Examples:

720. That's really helpful for me to hear.

721. I really feel like I understand you much better now.

722. It sounds like you are aware of a number of big factors that promote your positive changes.

723. You seem to be getting a stronger grip on the problem.

724. It sounds like you have a new insight into how to change your predicament.

725. If I hear you right you have more control over how to respond to others in that situation.

726. Let me see if I have this right . . . you are now aware of the changes you need to make in order to be happier.

727. So all in all you have a lot more direction in your life than a few weeks ago.

728. It makes sense that at this point you would be getting in touch with that aspect of your life.

729. You have come a long way since we started seeing one another. You really have worked hard at understanding the problem, and it sounds like you have a much better fix on how to overcome such an obstacle.

730. What I am guessing, based on what you just said, is that you have come to a better understanding of life in general and yourself in particular.

731. It sounds as if you are really finding meaning in life right now.

732. If I understand what you are telling me, you have become much better at enjoying life and connecting with others.

733. Having heard you say that things are going better in your life reminds me of the power of a person to overcome life's difficulties.

Providing Feedback

Approach aligned with: Universal skill

Purpose: To help the client further understand how they are being perceived by others. This skill is also used to help the therapist clarify what she is experiencing in the therapeutic relationship.

What the therapist does: The therapist tells the client what she is experiencing in the session in regard to the client's behaviors, feelings, attitudes, or statements.

Examples:

734. I just noticed how you seemed to relax your jaw muscles when you talked about that experience.

735. You and I have been sitting here in silence after what you said a few minutes ago . . . I notice that we are having trouble getting started again.

736. This week seems very different to me . . . in the past we have had trouble starting the session and yet this week we have already addressed several issues key to you.

737. You said you wanted me to give you some feedback on how you are coming across right now. I experience you as being angry with me for saying that.

738. I must share with you right now that I am really not sure what we are talking about. It seems that we have decided to talk about something other than the topic at hand.

739. I would like to ask your permission to give you some direct feedback right now. Is that okay? Okay, then I want you to know that when I hear you say how much that hurts you and see the look on your face as being one of pain and anguish, I really have a strong sense of how deeply this affects you.

740. When you say that it really doesn't matter what happens, I experience that as a suggestion that what we do together here is not relevant to you. That it really doesn't matter.

741. You asked me for some feedback about your progress in therapy. I want you to know that I have been impressed by your desire to continue to grow and develop along with your gumption and assertiveness in getting your needs met.

Immediacy

Approach aligned with: Universal skill

Purpose: To provide the client with feedback about how the therapist is experiencing the session, the client, or the story of the client. This feedback and therapist response should be anchored in the moment, not previous material.

What the therapist does: The therapist gives a statement that reflects his own response to something happening in the session at that time.

Examples:

742. When I hear you say that, I feel I can understand you better.

743. As we sit here, I am aware of your mounting frustration and, in turn, I feel frustrated as well.

744. The happier you appear, the more I experience joy and excitement.

745. Right here and right now we are having a difficult time communicating.

746. It makes a lot of sense that you report you are not sure about that, I too am rather confused about the scenario as well. In fact, I'm a little confused about this session right now.

747. As you were talking, my reaction to you was that of a child listening to a parent lecture her about right and wrong.

748. I'm experiencing you as angry right now. Is that accurate?

749. When you say you are happy with that, I can't help but feel happy for you as well because of all the effort and work you've put into it.

750. You said that people think of you as being standoffish. Right now I am experiencing you as being very genuine and not standoffish.

751. As you sit in my office and cry, I must share with you that I have a sense of loss for never meeting your husband. It sounds like he was a wonderful man.

752. I am experiencing great discomfort in the direction of conversation. I feel as though we have both decided to not talk about the core issue here.

753. I am getting the impression that right now you feel good about the direction your life is heading. I feel good about that as well.

754. As we start this week, I want you to know that I am experiencing excitement as I notice how good of a mood you are in.

Providing Information

Approach aligned with: Universal skill

Purpose: To provide factual knowledge to the session. This technique is used when the therapist is knowledgeable about a subject and has pertinent information to share.

What the therapist does: The therapist gives a direct statement of fact.

Examples:

755. It takes most students at least four years to complete college.

756. There are thousands of four-year college programs to choose from.

757. Most people who complete suicides have had a previous attempt.

758. Some studies show that the amount of sunlight you receive may affect your brain chemistry.

759. Some medications are used for both anxiety and depression.

760. The school policy is that after ten missed classes, the student has to submit a written plan of attendance before getting back into class.

761. In general, people in Western culture change their career path at least seven times over their life span.

762. Most accommodations for persons with disabilities cost less than fifty dollars.

763. Your insurance will pay, at least initially, for the first four sessions only.

764. As a certified school therapist, I have received specialized training in working with school students.

765. College courses are numbered to identify the level of student who should take each course. The higher the first number, the more advanced a course is.

766. If you decide to take a study hall this semester, you will be one-half a credit behind for graduation in two years. You can make that up in summer school or by taking English II next fall.

767. This interest inventory has been used for over thirty years and has correlation coefficients that indicate these areas are more closely aligned with these.

768. There are fewer people killed each year by rattlesnake bites than are killed by lightning.

Self-disclosure

Approach aligned with: Universal skill

Purpose: To provide the client with information about the therapist. When you self-disclose, it should be to establish greater rapport, humanize a client's experience, or promote greater insight and learning by the client. Self-disclosures should not change the direction of the session to be about the therapist instead of the client.

What the therapist does: The therapist makes a statement about something from her past that aligns with what has been discussed in the session.

Examples:

769. I have suffered great loss as well.
770. I have always had a desire to be a professional athlete as well.
771. I have some difficulty crying in public also.
772. When you mentioned that you felt happy about getting good grades this term, I remembered what it was like the first, and only, time I made the dean's list.
773. You talked about feeling bad about what you did. I too have had times when I did things I was not proud of.
774. I too have felt uncertain about what to do next.
775. I have difficulty in large groups as well. It does seem a bit uncomfortable at first.
776. I am different for having met you. I feel more in touch with my own feelings.
777. My family of origin has a history with alcohol as well.
778. I have worked with a number of different clients who have talked about being depressed.
779. I too know what it is like to have a great loss in life. My mother passed away when I was very young.
780. Just like you, and many others, I struggle with finding out who I am and what the world around me is about.
781. In my life, I have always had a desire to be something important through helping others.
782. I have a granddaughter named Meghan.
783. It seems that you are interested in knowing some things about me. I am okay to share some with you but feel that we need to keep a focus on why you are here. In response to your question, yes I am married, and I do not have any children.

Therapist's Feelings

Approach aligned with: Play therapy

Purpose: To share the therapist's current feelings and responses to actions and play by the child. Used in combination with Child's Feelings, Child's Content of Play, and Therapist's Content of Play to offer the child a play-by-play of the session.

What the therapist does: The therapist shares his feelings in direct and succinct statements.

Examples:

784. I am happy to see you today.

785. I am feeling cold right now.

786. I feel glad that you have decided to let me play with you.

787. I'm feeling unsure as to what you want me to be—the tiger or the bear.

788. It is exciting for me to talk with you.

789. When I play with this sandbox, I really enjoy it.

790. I'm feeling a bit unsure about your family too.

791. I feel confused about what we are doing with these toys too.

792. I get upset when people just reach out and grab the toy I was playing with.

793. I am happy for you that you have decided to talk with me about this.

794. I have a feeling that things will get better for you and your family.

795. It makes me sad when parents fight.

796. I feel strong when I lift things this big.

797. I like playing with paint.

798. I enjoy playing with cars.

799. The sand feels good in my hands.

800. I don't like the way that toy sounds.

801. I really have fun playing with Play-Doh.

802. Right now I feel tired.

803. As we are playing right now, I feel frustrated by these pictures.

804. I am having trouble cutting on the line. It makes me mad.

805. I am happy.

806. I am sad.

807. I am excited.

Therapist's Content of Play

Approach aligned with: Play therapy

Purpose: To make overt what the therapist is doing while engaged in play with the child. Used in conjunction with Therapist's Feelings, Child's Content of Play, and Child's Feelings.

What the therapist does: The therapist makes direct statements about what she is doing regarding play with the child.

Examples:

808. I am baking a pie.
809. I am helping you draw a picture.
810. I am just sitting here waiting for my next instruction.
811. I am mixing the paint together.
812. I finished sculpting the animals out of clay.
813. I'm picking up the toys.
814. I am getting the toys out of the box.
815. I am talking on the phone to a toy on the other end.
816. I am making animal sounds.
817. I am placing the crayons back in the box.
818. I opened the box.
819. I hit the drum.
820. I am standing up.
821. I moved over to play with this toy.
822. I lifted up the lid.
823. I am answering the phone.
824. I am making a picture of my family.
825. I moved the stuffed animal.
826. I am writing something down.
827. I am walking over to the sand tray.
828. I'm talking on the phone.
829. I put these stuffed animals together.
830. I am watching you play with those things.
831. I am fixing this toy.
832. I am baking.
833. Right now I am looking for a new toy.
834. My hands are working hard to sculpt this clay.
835. I am sitting in my chair drawing a picture of the room.
836. Okay, now I'm helping you put this together.

PRACTICE EXERCISES

Write your response, label the skill or skills used, then indicate your purpose for saying what you said.

Client: Well, I guess you got my message that I filed for bankruptcy last Tuesday. I really feel like I failed both my family and my employees.

Response 1 _____

_____

_____

Client: We've been talking about having sex, but I don't know if I'm ready yet.

Response 2 _____

_____

_____

Client: When I was a child I was afraid of dark places. Last night I had a dream that I was lost and it was dark. I woke up really scared and told my husband. He just rolled over and said go back to sleep. I really wanted him to hold me.

Response 3 _____

_____

_____

Client: I really feel like I am getting a lot out of coming here.

Response 4 _____

_____

_____

Client: I really don't know what to talk about. How do we start?

Response 5 _____

_____

_____

CHAPTER 9

Therapist's Actions

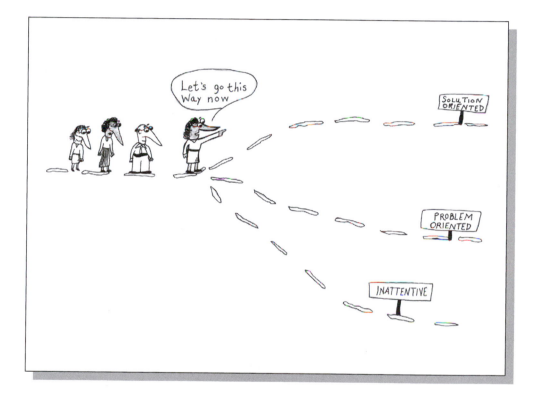

While totally committed to helping the client develop insight into her behaviors, the therapist must still make conscious choices regarding how the individual or group process is developing. In making those evaluations, the therapist may act consciously to move the focus of the session from one topic to another, or, in group work, from one group member to another. Sensitivity and experience are pluses here.

Holding the Focus

Approach aligned with: Universal skill

Purpose: To purposefully maintain the discussion on a singular subject.

What the therapist does: The therapist works to keep the client or clients from moving off of the subject and onto another topic. The client is asked to remain concentrated on the topic at hand.

Examples:

837. I want to go right back to what we were just talking about. Can you tell me more about the situation?

838. It seems as though you want to move to another topic, but I would like to hear some more about the reason you came for therapy, to help me get a better handle on how to help you.

839. Okay, going back for a minute, what was her motivation in writing you out of the will?

840. It appears as though you are having a strong reaction to this topic, but I want to stick with it for a little while longer.

841. I have noticed that each time we start to talk about getting in trouble with teachers, you make a joke and start talking about something else. I would like for us together to stay focused on the trouble you're having with teachers.

842. Going back to where we were a moment ago, you said pain. Can you tell me more about that?

843. I am aware that sometimes clients move away from subjects that are particularly troubling. I believe you have done just that. How can I help us get back on topic?

844. As a group, we have drifted away from sharing the connections we feel with one another. Does anyone have a hypothesis or explanation as to why we might be doing that?

845. Each time we approach the issue of loss in this group, the subject is quickly changed. Let's talk for a minute about loss without changing the subject.

846. You are a strong family—that is for sure. I noticed that as we started to talk about how others might have to change if Alexa decided to start going to school regularly the subject quickly moved to sports. Can we go back and address the changes that will be necessary for the family in order to help Alexa meet her goal?

Drawing Out

Approach aligned with: Group therapy, Family therapy

Purpose: To incorporate silent or quiet members of the group to provide more information for the group to hear.

What the therapist does: The therapist asks silent or quiet members to speak with either the entire group or certain members about things that are on their minds.

Examples:

847. Tariq, I would like to hear what you have been thinking about the last few minutes.

848. Chonca, you have been very quiet this week. It would be helpful if you would share with the group something you have been thinking about this session.

849. Moises, I noticed that when Daisy started talking a half hour ago, you became very quiet. Is there something that you wanted to share with the group right now about what you are experiencing?

850. Darin, I want you to pick out the person you feel most comfortable with right now and express something to them.

851. I am aware of how quiet you have been for the last few weeks. I think that silence has had an effect on the group. It might help all of us to know what the silence is about for you.

852. I have been talking a lot this week . . . so too have Aaron and Tom. I wonder, Michelle, if you could add anything to our conversation right now—what would it be?

853. We need to hear from other members of the group right now . . . Mike, Kim, and Steve have been leading the discussion—how about another voice?

854. Carl, you were talking a lot earlier. I wonder what happened that has kept you from talking. What, if anything, would you like to share with the group right now?

855. I saw you react to what she said. Can you put into words what you were feeling in that moment?

856. I have really enjoyed the group so far this week, but I am concerned that you have not said anything, Lee. What would you like the other group members to hear?

Joining

Approach aligned with: Family therapy

Purpose: To couple up with the client or clients in an attempt to form a "team" to defeat the problem. In individual therapy this is similar to developing rapport. In couples or family therapy the therapist has the choice to join one member, several family members, or the entire system.

What the therapist does: The therapist makes a statement or asks a question that signals to the client that he is aligned with the client.

Examples:

857. You and I have been working on this problem for two sessions now. What is it that we have been able to do to help defeat it so far?

858. I am not sure what you mean, Winston. Angela seems to be the one having trouble getting over the loss. You seem to be handling it very well.

859. Okay, so as I watch the two of you discuss this I am more and more aware of what the situation is. It seems that you, Ryan, are having a lot of trouble forgiving Ian for what he did.

860. So part of the family would like to deal with this issue by meeting as we have been doing each week. The other part of the family would like to handle it by stopping therapy. I tend to agree with Andy who said that things have started to get better as a result of the work we have done here.

861. It is apparent to me that when you say that "we" have done several things that have worked in our time together that "we" do make a good team against the depressive thing.

862. Matt, what can you and I do this week to help you get better control over your fear of talking in front of others?

863. What can we do this week as a team to help you cope with the loss?

864. What have we done in our time together that was effective or helpful in combating those troubling thoughts?

865. If I am understanding the family right now, you are all in agreement that Alvin needs to be cured. How is it that we can do such a thing without upsetting the family system?

866. Right now I have the sense that we are working together as a team to defeat this problem.

Protection

Approach aligned with: Group therapy

Purpose: To keep members of the group free of harm from others in the group or of too much information or feedback too quickly.

What the therapist does: The therapist maintains the safety of the client by diverting attention, changing the subject, refocusing the group attention, or removing the client from the hot seat.

Examples:

867. Marcia, you have heard a lot of new information in the last few minutes; I want to make sure that we don't overload you so I am going to shift the focus right now.

868. It sounds like Chris has heard enough right now. What else can we focus on right now?

869. I am not sure that Sue needs any more feedback on this subject right now.

870. Mary Jane, it looks like you have had enough for now . . . right?

871. Lisa, I am sure that we could continue this conversation, but it appears to me that Linda has had her fill.

872. Am I correct, Julius, that we might want to change topics right now?

873. I feel the need to start the group moving in a slightly different direction right now.

874. That is a lot of information we just gave Nick. Let's let him take it all in and move in another direction for now.

875. Anne, you are really upset right now and seem to be putting a lot of the blame and anger you have on several group members. I think as a group we need to take a break and collect ourselves.

876. If you decide to hit him, you will be removed from this group.

877. Right now we seem to have a laser beam focused on Mirian. Part of my job is to make sure that no one group member gets hurt in here from too much confrontation. Let's take a step back and refocus the group back to talking about the interaction between Kareem and Jean-Marie.

878. I am experiencing this group as unsafe right now. That is because I see how much direct feedback we are giving to Austin. Let's shift gears and slow things down a bit.

Unbalancing

Approach aligned with: Family therapy

Purpose: To disrupt the functioning of the family and make them change into a new way of functioning.

What the therapist does: The therapist aligns with one subsystem over another. The therapist may align with an individual or small group.

Examples:

879. So as I watch you I am struck by how strongly the two groups feel about this issue. I tend to agree with this group that there is hope for the future in this regard.

880. Billy, Brad, and Sterling seem to be interested in getting you to follow along with what they are saying regarding family meetings. I tend to agree with you though. Maybe now isn't the best time to start such measures.

881. It seems that we have two different trains of thought in regard to how to improve the group. One is to focus more on here-and-now issues, the other is to take more time to hear individual stories from the past. I align myself with those interested in focusing on here-and-now issues.

882. If you are interested in what I think, I believe that the family should plan a large get-together for this weekend.

883. It must be really tough to always be excluded from the group decisions, especially when you have some really good insight and facts to be considered by the rest of the group.

884. It makes sense to me that the family would be polarized on this issue. I can understand what this side is saying, but find myself aligning much more with this other group on this particular topic.

885. So we have three distinct and different groups with ideas of how to help the family function better in the morning. One idea is to assign bathroom times, another idea is to use the first-come-first-served method, and then Jake here has a third idea that the family should work together in terms of who needs it first, second, and so forth. I agree with Jake on this issue.

886. Wow, it seems as though the rest of the family is really coming down on you about how you handled that in school. That must be really hard when they do that. This seems unfair to me.

Shifting the Focus

Approach aligned with: Universal skill

Purpose: To move the topic to something that might be more productive or therapeutic for the client. It is used when the client seems to be rambling on about something or avoiding something.

What the therapist does: The therapist uses verbal and/or nonverbal communication to move the client from one topic to another.

Examples:

887. Going back, you said a while ago that your mother was coming to town?

888. Wait a second, I think we just skipped over something a few moments ago. You mentioned that you were thinking you might not have a job in a few weeks . . . then you went into a conversation about time management. Could we go back to the part about losing your job?

889. Okay, okay, you have given me a lot of information right now. Let's go back a step and talk about what brought you in here, your concern for your eating habits.

890. So how does that relate to your goal of being more independent?

891. I heard what you just said about having a good time on vacation, but I am curious how it relates to anger management.

892. In the time we have left today I want to focus on your desire to have your family function in a more peaceful way.

893. Obviously you are having a strong emotional reaction to what we have been talking about. I want to shift gears here for a minute and ask you about your thoughts regarding the matter. From a neutral position how do you see the relationship?

894. We have been talking about a lot of different things today. What specifically would you like to talk about in regard to the issue?

895. The two of you have been expressing how interesting it is to watch people on the subway. I agree it is interesting, but I wonder if we are moving away from the issue you came in here with, lack of sex in the marriage, because somehow we got too close to something that is painful.

PRACTICE EXERCISES

Write your response, label the skill or skills used, then indicate your purpose for saying what you said.

Client: We've been together for two years now. It seems like we should know how to read each other, but there are times when we don't seem to agree on anything.

Response 1 _____

_____

Client: Yeah, I'm doing better with not yelling out in class. Hey, did you see the game last night?

Response 2 _____

_____

Client: I don't know why I have to come here every week. My original therapist was much better at understanding what I was saying and what we should talk about. This is a waste of time.

Response 3 _____

_____

Client: (a couple talking to one another) Amy: He always does that, he makes me feel like I have nothing of value to say and that I am crazy for wanting to work on our relationship. Todd: No, you are the one who blows things out of proportion. I just don't think we need to talk about everything.

Response 4 _____

_____

Client: I feel really strange talking to someone about this. I never share things like this with anyone.

Response 5 _____

_____

Pure Imagination

For many years therapists have recognized the presence and power of imagery and useful mind images as they relate to personal mental health and psychological balance. This chapter includes several skills devoted to getting clients to tap into such valuable personal resources.

Camera Check

Approach aligned with: Cognitive-Behavioral therapy

Purpose: To have the client objectify the content of the session and make overt the thoughts the client is having rather than focusing on emotions.

What the therapist does: The therapist asks the client to envision and describe what a camera might be seeing in the moment of the session.

Examples:

896. What would a camera be picking up right now?

897. If a camera where pointed down on us what images would it be recording?

898. If we were taping this session what moment would the camera pick up that really stands out?

899. If we had a Polaroid of this moment in the session what would be in the picture?

900. What image would a camera pick up from the last few minutes?

901. If we had a series of pictures of this session what images would we see on those pictures?

902. How would the person behind the camera see what has happened in the last few minutes of this session?

903. How would someone taking a picture of your family in that moment view it? What would be in the picture?

904. When you and your husband are fighting what would be in the image if a picture were snapped in the heat of the moment?

905. When you get in trouble what would the camera see in regard to how you handle it? What image would be present on the film?

906. Let's imagine for a moment that a camera was catching all of this discussion. But, this is a special camera—it takes pictures and then puts them together in an overall picture. What would that overall picture have in it for this session?

907. We have seen each other for six sessions now. I am curious. What would the difference be, if we took pictures from the first session and then compared them to what a camera would be seeing right now?

908. How might a camera pick up the difference between when you are down and when you are happy, like right now?

Creative Imagery

Approach aligned with: Cognitive-Behavioral therapy

Purpose: To provide a warm-up exercise to get clients prepared for further psychodrama experiences.

What the therapist does: The therapist asks the client to imagine either neutral or pleasant images as a means of promoting a spontaneous creative feeling.

Examples:

909. Now I want you to close your eyes and imagine a place that is warm and safe, a place you like to go to.

910. Imagine for a few moments an imaginary place that you would like to visit.

911. Picture for a few seconds here the place you imagine when you are relaxed and want to daydream about some place you have never been.

912. Go to a place in your mind where you are not judged or expected to meet timelines . . . a place that you can relax and kick up your heels and feel warm and safe.

913. As we start today, I want you to take a few minutes and go to a place in your mind that is neither positive nor negative.

914. Center your thoughts on a neutral place in your mind. What does it look like, smell like, feel like, and so on.

915. Let's take some time and go to a place that has a positive feeling for you.

916. Close your eyes and go to a happy, warm, safe place in your mind.

917. Close your eyes and go to a neutral place.

918. In the first few minutes of this week's session I want you to take some time and relax and get into a place in your mind that is warm and safe.

919. I want you to close your eyes and find your center . . . feel yourself becoming balanced and comfortable.

920. Before we progress, I want to have you relax your mind by going to a positive place. Take a few moments and find a place in your mind's eye that is warm, safe, relaxing, and enjoyable.

921. Sit back and relax for a moment and take yourself to a place that you associate with being positive.

Early Recollections

Approach aligned with: Individual Psychology

Purpose: To hear about the current life situations a person is having through displacement onto past events.

What the therapist does: The therapist asks the client to share some memories from childhood, before the age of six or seven. The therapist can also program or prescribe certain actions, thoughts, or behaviors by asking the client to think about certain situations that arose in childhood. The therapist listens closely for themes in the early recollections that reveal the client's felt place in life, feelings about self, and feelings for others.

Examples:

922. Think back to before you were six years old. What memories do you have?

923. Can you tell me something that happened to you, say, before the age of six or seven?

924. What memories do you have from your childhood . . . say before the age of six, when you were active with others?

925. What memories do you have from your past when you felt as though you were in charge of things . . . say before the age of seven?

926. Can you give me several images or pictures that are in your mind's eye from your childhood?

927. Going back to your childhood. What was your house like before you moved?

928. You said your parents divorced when you were eight. What images or memories do you have in your mind from before that time?

929. Thinking back a long time ago . . . say, when you were five or six, what images or memories come to mind for you?

930. What early recollections do you have from your childhood?

931. When you were a kid, did you ever have moments when you felt really connected to others?

932. Tell me about a time when you were a child and you found yourself being helpful to others.

Focused Imagery

Approach aligned with: Universal skill

Purpose: To help the client move ideas or thoughts into actions. To have the client not just talk about doing something different but actually see it happening.

What the therapist does: The therapist asks the client to imagine making a behavioral change and see it happening in the client's mind's eye. The therapist can also ask the client to imagine doing more of the same if the technique is working.

Examples:

933. Okay, so now we have talked about what your life might be like if you were to change how you responded to your mother in those moments. I want you now to close your eyes and imagine the conversation you will have. How will it be different when you do this?

934. So you want to be more assertive in moments when people ask a lot of you at work. Imagine for a second that someone has just asked you to do something not in your job description. How will you respond in an assertive way to such a request?

935. You said that it seemed to work well when you took a few minutes away from the situation to process your own thoughts. Take a few minutes right now and imagine doing more of that. What will the outcome be if you choose to do this?

936. Louis, I heard you say that you wanted to do more of the same in regard to keeping your room clean. What will be the consequences, both positive and negative, if you keep your room clean on a regular basis? Close your eyes and imagine this were to happen.

937. We have discussed your wanting to be less judgmental of others. So right now I want you to respond to some of my statements without being critical or judgmental. And as you said, I want you to use more empathy and understanding of my viewpoint.

938. As we have been talking, I am impressed by your desire to make such a definitive change in your life. So right now, I want you to imagine what your world will be like when you make such a change. How will others respond to you?

Logical Consequences

Approach aligned with: Universal skill

Purpose: This skill is used to provide the client with a chance to explore what will happen, both good and bad, when the client changes a thought or behavior.

What the therapist does: The therapist helps the client assess what the pros and cons of the actions they described might be.

Examples:

939. If you decide to change in that way how will people view you differently?

940. What are the negative aspects to asserting your opinion?

941. So it is only logical that by you changing your attitude, those around you will change theirs as well.

942. How happy will your family be to see you acting differently under those circumstances?

943. What are the pros and cons to such changes?

944. If you change back, what will the negative effects be? The positive ones?

945. You have thought about the consequences of doing that. What are some of those consequences?

946. How will your mom and dad feel about you moving out?

947. Who will be happiest for you about this change? Who will be upset about this change?

948. As you start to act differently, what are the long-term benefits and potential problems?

949. What are the pros and cons to making this change in your life right now?

950. Okay, so we have talked about what you would like to have different in your life. You said you want to be happier and feel less stress. But I am curious . . . what will be the logical outcome if you have less stress in your life?

951. Changes can sometimes upset the entire family system. They aren't always aware of why you would like to behave differently. Let's talk for a while about what might be good and what might be bad if you decide to continue on this new path.

952. Sometimes it is important to consider what effect, if any, we will have on people around us if we give up a problem we have carried for a long time. What are the pros and cons to putting this problem down and moving on with your life?

Progressive Relaxation

Approach aligned with: Cognitive-Behavioral therapy

Purpose: To teach the client a sequence of thoughts and behaviors that arouse a relaxed state of mind and body.

What the therapist does: The therapist walks the client through self-statements accompanied by relaxation and tension of specific muscles (". . ." indicates a pause until the behavior is complete).

Examples:

953. Get in a relaxed position with nothing in your body crossed . . . uncross your legs . . . uncross your fingers . . . your arms . . . focus on your breathing . . . pay attention to the air going in and going out . . . get complete control of your breath . . . breathe in . . . now breath out . . . .

954. Now focus on your toes . . . feel the tension in your toes . . . make your toes tight and hard and firm . . . now relax your toes . . . make them soft and warm and relaxed . . . make your toes tight and hard and firm . . . now relax your toes . . . make them soft and warm and relaxed.

955. Now move to your feet. Feel the tension in your feet . . . make your feet tight and hard and firm . . . now relax your feet . . . make them soft and warm and relaxed . . . make your feet tight and hard and firm . . . now relax your feet . . . make them soft and warm.

956. Focus on your breathing and feel the air going in and out, with each breath you are feeling more relaxed and calm.

957. Now focus on your calves . . . feel the tension in your calves . . . make your calves tight and hard and firm . . . now relax your calves . . . make your calves tight and hard and firm . . . now relax your calves . . . make them soft and warm and relaxed.

958. Okay, now focus on your thighs. Feel the tension in your quads . . . make your thighs tight and hard and firm . . . now relax your thighs, make them soft and warm and relaxed . . . make your thighs tight and hard and firm . . . now relax your thighs . . . make them soft and warm and relaxed.

959. Now focus on your hips. Feel the tension in your hips. Now make your hips tight and hard and firm . . . now relax your hips, make them soft and warm and relaxed. Now make your hips tight and hard and firm . . . now relax your hips, make them soft and warm.

Note: This procedure is followed for the rest of the body.

Imaginal Treatment

Approach aligned with: Cognitive-Behavioral therapy

Purpose: To help the client be successful in a difficult situation, overcome issues, and/or achieve in the face of adversity or anxiety.

What the therapist does: The therapist helps the client learn to use his imagination to overpower negative, self-defeating, or anxiety-provoking thoughts.

Examples:

960. Okay, so you said that you have great difficulty talking to women. Right now I want you to close your eyes and picture yourself approaching a woman. Now imagine yourself successfully starting a conversation with her.

961. As you start to think about approaching your boss and confronting him, I want you to say what you feel. Okay, I hear you saying you feel nervous and anxious. So now I want you to practice some of your relaxation techniques. Control your breathing, slow down your pace, and relax.

962. If I hear you correctly, you are saying that when you picture your grandmother you feel calm and a sense of warmth and comfort, right? Okay, then, as you start to imagine the setting of the problem at school, picture your grandmother and see what effect that has on your emotional response.

963. I am hearing you say that you want to stop yourself from doing that, but can't seem to do so in the moment. So I want you to imagine a huge stop sign in your head. Get the picture of the biggest stop sign ever made. Now focus intently on it. What things do you notice regarding how it is shaped . . . the exact color of the red . . . the outline of the letters. (Pause) Now that you have that clear picture in your head, the next time you start doing what you know you should not do, and do not want to do, flash your stop sign in your head and hold it there until you decide to stop the behavior.

964. I heard you say in several sessions that you want to listen more intently and show more affection for your wife. Take a few moments and get into a calm place in your mind where you can actually imagine that happening. Now, picture it happening. What are you doing differently? How do you feel about yourself?

PRACTICE EXERCISES

Write your response, label the skill or skills used, then indicate your purpose for saying what you said.

Client: When I think about being around all of my relatives, I just get all tense and scared. The last time I saw them I was very different. Things have happened since that have made it hard to get along. I think most of them hate me.

Response 1 _____

_____

_____

Client: I just think back and remember how good it was when we all got along. You know, before the accident.

Response 2 _____

_____

_____

Client: There is nothing I want to do more than not be afraid of being alone at night. But it seems like the more I think about it, the stronger the feeling is. I think I will just have to deal with this for the rest of my life.

Response 3 _____

_____

_____

Client: I've just been having a lot of trouble with my parents. They don't want me to have a life. It's like they want me to suffer in front of my friends rather than have fun and enjoy things.

Response 4 _____

_____

_____

Client: Am I supposed to feel good about my condition? I hate when people look at me and say she is so fat and ugly. Am I supposed to ignore all of that and just be happy?

Response 5 _____

_____

_____

CHAPTER 11

....

Waves in Motion

In this chapter, we present techniques that can be used to help the client move into action. However, special care must be taken in using this set of skills. These techniques do not confer a license to give advice, tell someone how to act, or what to do. Well-anchored Waves-in-Motion skills should originate from within the client. Until a therapist has developed a clear sense of how these skills work, she should probably utilize them only under the direct supervision of a therapist who has had experience using such skills.

Challenges

Approach aligned with: Group therapy

Purpose: To provide the client with an opportunity within group to make use of suggestions, new insights, or directions provided by others to change their behavior.

What the therapist does: The therapist suggests that the client has a chance to make a change right in the moment with the new information provided by group and offers a safe chance for them to do it.

Examples:

965. Now that the group has given you some ideas about how to be more assertive with others are you willing to use some of their suggestions with Jane?

966. Okay, you've heard from another group member about how she deals with anger, and I'm noticing you getting angry right now. Rather than wait until you get home, what can you use from the group's suggestions right now?

967. What would you like to use from those suggestions right now in this moment?

968. Just as an experiment, the next time you start to feel alone in this group, pick out one of the things the other group members talked about and use it. Let us know how this works out.

969. The next time you feel like you need to raise your voice, I'd like you to practice your breathing for thirty seconds. Then in a normal-toned voice, assert your true feelings to the individual.

970. In the event that you try to use seduction as a way of getting your way with another group member, I want them to point out what they are experiencing and then have you choose another way of trying to move them.

971. As you indicated during the first group, you have trouble connecting with others. I want you to pick out a group member and use some of the things presented by this group to try to form a deeper connection with them.

972. I would like to issue a challenge to the entire group. We have been talking in general about making changes in our own lives. I want us to change how this group is functioning, and rather than just talking about those changes I want us to actually do them here in the moment.

Conjoint Family Drawing

Approach aligned with: Family therapy

Purpose: To have the client(s) acquire a better understanding of their family and the structure of the family.

What the therapist does: The therapist asks each family member to draw a picture of their family as they see them. Once the pictures are drawn, the therapist facilitates a discussion in which the family shares their perceptions and meanings of their drawings.

Examples:

973. Okay, now I want each of you to draw your family as you see them. Use any colors or symbols you would like.

974. Draw a picture as you envision yourself and your entire family.

975. Please take a minute and draw a picture of what your family looks like.

976. For the next few minutes I want each of you to work independently and draw and color a picture of what your family looks like to you.

977. We each have a picture in our head of what our family looks like. Take a few minutes and draw the picture in your head of your family.

978. Now that you have drawn your family, what similarities do you see among all the pictures?

979. Look at all these drawings. What is different among them?

980. How are these pictures the same? Different?

981. What would you like to see in each of these pictures?

982. If we combined all of the pictures, what would the overall picture look like?

983. I want each of you to pick a color for each family member and then draw a picture of a typical day in your household. When all of you have finished we will take a few minutes to talk about each picture.

984. Okay, so as we get started this week, let's all grab some colors and take some time to think and then draw a picture of your family. Make it a day when things are going really well and the problem is not present. Be as detailed as possible.

Empty Chair Technique

Approach aligned with: Gestalt therapy

Purpose: To promote further growth and insight by the client through expressing himself in a way he might not otherwise choose. It encourages the client to have an imaginary discussion with someone he needs to share something with.

What the therapist does: The therapist asks the client to express sentiments and thoughts to a group or family member who is not present. It can also be used to allow clients to speak to persons unavailable to join them in the session, such as deceased family members. The primary aim for this technique is to encourage the client to work through unfinished thoughts and/or feelings associated with another person.

Examples:

985. Alexa, I want you to talk to this empty chair as if you were speaking to Jacob.

986. Ryan, you mentioned your mother on several occasions, I want you to act as if she was here sitting in this chair right now. Tell her how you feel.

987. Mary Jane, this request will sound a bit goofy but I want you to talk to this chair as if your grandma was here and able to hear you.

988. Ian, let's take the next few minutes and try something. It will sound a bit strange at first, but I want you to talk to this chair as if Marcia was sitting in it. Tell her what you think of last week's group.

989. I want everyone in the group to talk to Thom's empty chair as if he was here. Tell him what you think of him missing his third group session.

990. Let's go around the group and hear what all of us have to say to Charlotte. Talk to her chair as if she were sitting here right now.

991. You have mentioned the loss of your daughter. I want you to take a minute and pretend that she was sitting here with us and verbalize what you are feeling right now to her.

992. In the next few minutes of group we are going to try something new. As you may have noticed, Don did not join us this week. I am wondering what we all have to say to him. Rather than wait until next week, let's pretend that he is here with us and talk to his chair telling him what we are thinking right now.

Icebreaker

Approach aligned with: Group therapy

Purpose: To get clients started in the process of talking with one another.

What the therapist does: The therapist asks the clients to engage in an activity that promotes discussion and communication. Clients are instructed to take part in an activity that is not threatening and asks them to reveal only a little of themselves.

Examples:

993. I would like to go around the circle and have everyone give us a few statements about what brought them to group.

994. Okay, now I want you to think about your favorite color. Now pair up with someone and share both what it is and why you think so.

995. Now, let's try something else. I want you to pair up and share the responses you wrote down to the questions I asked a few minutes ago.

996. I want you to share something with the group as the ball of string gets passed to you. Hold on to the ball of string and unwind. You can pass the ball to anyone you want after you have shared something with the group. Keep hold of the string though.

997. Okay, for this exercise, I want to break you up by eye color. Blue eyes over here, brown here, green here. Now, working as a group, come up with five great things about having the eye color you have.

998. Before we get started, I want us to each take a minute and introduce ourselves. Rather than doing it for the entire group, however, you will introduce yourself to each person as we all mingle around the room.

999. Take a minute and think about your favorite type of music. When you are ready, share it with the group, and perhaps a bit about why you think you like that music best.

1000. Of course this is a group about controlling our anger. But before we get into the stuff, let's take a minute to introduce ourselves. Why doesn't each of us give the group their name, occupation, and something interesting about themselves.

1001. Before we get rolling, I want everyone to take a minute and introduce the person next to them. Let's take some time to get to know that person.

Group Observing Group (Fishbowl Procedure)

Approach aligned with: Group therapy

Purpose: To have a section of the group observe and then report on what they observed happening in the group. Provides a meta-perspective with new insight and awareness for the rest of the group to hear.

What the therapist does: The therapist breaks the group into two groups. One group sits outside of the other group and observes the interactions of the group within the "fishbowl." The therapist then facilitates a discussion of what was observed and experienced.

Examples:

1002. I want Danny, Amiri, and Colin to arrange yourselves so that you are sitting outside of the main group. For the next twenty minutes I want the three of you to observe the main group's interactions. Notice who is talking a lot, who is talking a little, what is being discussed, who changes subjects, et cetera.

1003. Now, as you can see, we have broken the group into two subgroups. For the first thirty minutes of this week's session, the outside group will observe and then report on everything that goes on in the inner group. We will then switch positions and repeat the process.

(once the observations have been made)

1004. What was your overall understanding of how this group was functioning?

1005. What surprised you the most about how the group functioned?

1006. Who was most active? Who was least active? What are your thoughts as to why this occurred?

1007. What new insights or knowledge can you offer to the group when we return to one large group?

1008. How was it that group members decided to talk about an issue?

1009. Which topics or issues that were explored seemed to cause the most problems for the group?

1010. During what moment did you most want to say something to the group?

Pat on the Back

Approach aligned with: Group therapy

Purpose: To provide group members with positive feedback from other group members. Only clear, direct, positive comments are acceptable.

What the therapist does: The therapist asks clients to draw an outline of their hand on a piece of paper and then attach the paper to their back. Once the paper is secured on their back, group members go around and write positive comments on the other members' papers (on the hand).

Examples:

1011. Okay, as we close, I want everyone to grab a piece of paper and draw an outline of your hand on it. Now, take the paper and have someone tape it to your back. Now, I want you each to write something positive or constructive on the hands of everyone in the group.

1012. As we finish this week I want to try something a little bit odd. I want us each to do this . . . (therapist demonstrates how to draw the outline of the hand) . . . once you have done this, get someone to tape it on your back . . . then go around the room and write something positive on each person's hand.

1013. We deserve a pat on the back. Today you will get one! Here is how it works. Take a piece of paper and draw your hand. Then have it taped to your back. Then write something positive or constructive or both on each of the other group member's hands.

1014. Once again, I would like us to do the pat-on-the-back exercise to end group. But this time, I want you to anchor your comments on the last half of group, share something constructive or positive from the last half of this week's group.

1015. As we end the session, let's try the pat-on-the-back exercise as we did last week, only this time write something positive related to the nonverbal behavior you saw from each group member.

1016. We are going to try something different this week. I want everyone to take some time and think about the positive attributes each group member has. Once you have them, take these pieces of paper and tape and write down those attributes. Remember, only positives, and then tape it onto their back.

Pretend Technique

Approach aligned with: Family therapy

Purpose: To help the client see that a once involuntary problem can be controlled. This technique is similar to acting "as if" in Adlerian individual psychology.

What the therapist does: The therapist asks the client or clients to pretend to have the problem right in the session.

Examples:

1017. I want the two of you to fight as if you were at home and he had just said the wrong thing.

1018. Lenny, I want you to pretend that you have just received a bad grade on your paper. Act out what you are thinking and feeling.

1019. Now, as a family, you have been talking about the problem as if it was distant from you. I want to see what really happens in the moment of these morning rituals. I want you to act out what really happens when you get up in the morning. Who does and says what?

1020. You have given me a good description of the problem. Now I want to see you act it out, okay?

1021. I agree that the fighting has to stop. You are right that it does no one any good to hear such arguments, especially your kids. So, for now, to help us all see the power of this problem, I want you to pick a fight with one another. Let's see how these things get started.

1022. If right now, in this moment, you were to share your love for one another, what things might you say to express that? Can you pretend if only for a moment to do this?

1023. Okay, now I want to try something a bit different. I have heard you talk about what you would like to say to one another for half an hour. But what stands out to me is that we have the time and the opportunity to see what will happen if you decide to do this. So, let's take a few minutes and do just that. I want you to share what you would like with one another . . . pretending that this is not really real.

1024. That behavior seems to cause you a lot of trouble. I'd like to see what it is like when it emerges. Can you kind of act it out for me right now?

Role Playing

Approach aligned with: Universal skill

Purpose: To have the client practice behaviors that they might later want to incorporate into their real life.

What the therapist does: The therapist asks the client to act out what they want to see happen in a future situation. It can be directed by the therapist or directed by the client or a combination of both.

Examples:

1025. Okay, now that you have described the ideal person and identified some specific traits, I want you to pick one of the traits and practice it here in this session.

1026. I want you to act as if you were more like that person. How would you handle the situation you described earlier with your mother?

1027. I want you to function as someone you emulate in terms of dealing with people who are bossy.

1028. Let's take a few minutes and practice what it would be like to have the nerve to stand up to your boss. I will be your boss.

1029. So for the next few minutes, I think it would be worthwhile to practice these new behaviors you have described.

1030. You said that you think you are improving at talking with more eye contact and a louder voice. Let's take a few minutes and see how you do. I will monitor you and give you feedback.

1031. As you think about how you want to act differently in that situation, which aspect of showing more interest would you like to see? Let's practice that right now in the moment.

1032. I want you to pretend that you have the courage to tell people what you think. I will pretend to be your husband.

1033. In the next few minutes, I think it would help if you were to act as if you weren't mad about what he had done.

1034. Okay, you be Elisa and I will be Tom. How would you like to see the conversation go from your point of view?

1035. Okay, so for a moment I want you to imagine that we are different people. I will play the part of someone afraid to talk to people they don't know. You play the part of a stranger. Let's talk through how my character might overcome or cope with this fear and actually connect with the stranger.

Role Reversal

Approach aligned with: Universal skill

Purpose: To have the client act out the part of an alternative view of the world. This technique is used to help the client realize that things can be different and that she can act differently.

What the therapist does: The therapist asks the client to assume the position of the person or people most opposite of what she normally assumes. Special attention is paid to the client understanding the cognitive, emotional, and reactive positioning of the "other" type of person.

Examples:

1036. So you are normally assertive, I want you to act as if you are passive.

1037. I want you to do the opposite in this case . . . I want you to show a lot of feelings and emotions about the loss.

1038. You always seem to be the strong one in those types of situations. I want you to take a few minutes and act out the part of being the weak one.

1039. I am interested in having you experience this from the other side. I want you to pretend and instead of being extremely interested in everything she does, I want you to act aloof. Let's see how it feels.

1040. For a few minutes, I want you to act the complete opposite of how you normally would in relation to showing emotion.

1041. I want you to pretend that you have no fear of doing that. Act as if you are someone who does not fear closeness.

1042. I want you to play the part of someone opposite you in that way. So, rather than being extremely emotional, I want you to be extremely cognitive for a few moments.

1043. You are talking about wanting to act differently in that type of situation. I want you to now practice being different when confronted. Rather than getting defensive I want you to be open to the experience.

1044. Why don't you take a few minutes and reverse roles. Act like the person who is most opposite you in this type of scenario.

1045. I want you to try to be verbose rather than, as you put it, timid, for the next ten minutes.

Sculpting

Approach aligned with: Family therapy and Group therapy

Purpose: To provide the client with insight into relationships and understandings of others in a clearer and deeper way.

What the therapist does: The therapist asks the client to rearrange materials and people in the room to mimic his significant people. This movement is accomplished through the client's use of nonverbal techniques.

Examples:

1046. So now we have heard about how your coworkers function. Now I want you to arrange the group into a routine moment at work . . . but I want you to use only nonverbal communication.

1047. As we did last week, I want you to arrange your family in a way that best typifies the normal morning routine. Do not use words . . . use only hand signals and other nonverbal forms of communication.

1048. Now that we have heard a description of how you tend to function when confronted with that type of situation, I want you to take ten minutes or so and put the entire group to work portraying the individuals you previously described. You are not to use words or sounds of any kind to indicate to us what you want.

1049. Before we move to another topic I want to see what you are describing. Please take a minute and reenact what you were describing by placing your family into their appropriate positions. Do this without any talking.

1050. Like last week, I want you to sculpt a picture of what your words have described. Use the group at your disposal, but remember not to use any words—only hand gestures, body movements, and other means of communicating without talking.

1051. Okay, right now I want to have you try to act out the situation you just described. Take a look around the group and find the people who you most align with your family. Make use of the other materials in the room to develop the scene. What I want you to do is arrange the people and things in this room to resemble as best you can, the typical day in your family as you just described it. You have all the time you need to do this, and we will all try the best way we know how to help.

Serial Art Therapy

Approach aligned with: Play therapy

Purpose: To have the client use drawing as a means of healing. The art work alone is considered to be therapeutic.

What the therapist does: The therapist asks the child to draw a picture at each session. The therapist does not analyze the pictures, but rather allows the client to work through her own material at her own pace through the drawings. The drawings may be structured or unstructured.

Examples:

1052. Okay, Darryl, I want you to take a few minutes and draw a picture. Maybe you could draw your family at home.

1053. I want you to take the coloring materials I have here and draw me a picture of anything you want.

1054. Just like you did last week, I want you to go ahead and draw another picture.

1055. You know what time it is now. Right. It's time to draw another picture. Go ahead.

1056. Okay, so now I would like you to take some time and draw a picture of yourself at school. Include the people who are important to you.

1057. I want to see what you draw today. Go ahead and get started. This week though I want to see a picture of some of your family. You decide who is in the picture.

1058. Go ahead and pick out a picture from inside your head and use these coloring markers to draw and color it, okay?

1059. You made some different pictures last week. This week I want you to do some more drawings.

1060. Can you show your mom and I how well you draw? Go ahead and draw and color anything you would like.

1061. You can see what I am doing, right? I am drawing. Would you like to join me?

1062. So as we get started this week, I want you to take some time and work on some drawings. Pick out the materials you want to use and take this paper and go ahead. Whatever you want to draw is fine, and you have the entire time we have together to use for your art work.

Wheel of Influence

Approach aligned with: Family therapy

Purpose: To surface and highlight the connection an individual has with others. This provides insight into the strength of alliances with others and documents the role and function of others in the life of the client.

What the therapist does: The therapist asks the client to create a picture of the main people who have an influence on his life with themselves in the middle. The lines connecting the client with other people can be highlighted or darkened to indicate the varying amounts of influence.

Examples:

1063. So now that we have talked about your family and friends, I want you to take a few minutes and draw out a picture of who has a significant amount of influence on your life. Put yourself in the middle and shade the lines according to most and least influential people.

1064. Take a few minutes and draw out, in a circle with you in the middle, the most important people in your world. Shade lines heavier for those who have the strongest effect on your life.

1065. Among all the people you have ever known, pick out those who seem to have had the biggest effect on your life. Put yourself in the middle, and like spokes on a wheel, pencil in those people who stand out to you.

1066. Between now and next week I want you to complete a simple homework assignment. I want you to take this sheet of paper, write your name in the middle, and then, in a circle around your name, write the names of the people who have had the largest amount of influence on your life and who you are today.

1067. For homework this week, I want you to draw a diagram of the most influential people in your life, both presently and over the entire course of your life. Put yourself in the center and then write the names of those people you decided on around the perimeter with lines connecting you to them. Make the lines relative to one another by using darker or lighter strokes to indicate amount of influence.

Experimentation

Approach aligned with: Gestalt therapy

Purpose: To have the client do something rather than just talk about issues or troubles. Experiments can be either prescribed as homework or done right in the moment of the session. Experiments are used to help the client make connections among and between mind, body, and feelings.

What the therapist does: The therapist asks the client to continue doing something physical in the session, start doing something physical in the session, or complete an assignment at home that involves movement.

Examples:

1068. I can see that you are wringing your hands together like this (therapist shows the client). I would like you to continue to do that but even faster and with more effort.

1069. When you talk about your mother, you slouch in your chair. Can you slouch even more as we continue to talk about her?

1070. Tonight, and every night this week, I want you to do what you just did (shows the client a facial expression) when you think about the anger you have for the situation.

1071. Even as we sit here I am amazed at how you can talk about such a great loss and yet still smile. I would like you to smile even wider as we talk about it.

1072. You have said that every time you start to think about that, you stop whatever you are doing and sit down and start to eat. I would like you to do something very different next time. After having those thoughts and feelings and having sat down to eat, I want you to stand up and raise your hands directly over your head. Then I want you to write down how that one action makes you feel.

1073. You are doing this—shaking your head and fixing your hair— what does that mean? Can you tell me?

1074. I'm sure that it is important to you in some way that when you talk about your drinking you bite on your fingertips, but I do not know what it means. What are you trying to tell me?

1075. You motion over to the corner when you talk about being abused by your father. What is in the corner that you would like me to know about?

Psychodrama

Approach aligned with: Psychodrama

Purpose: To have the client in group reexperience her description of an event from the past. This technique is used to work with unfinished business. In this way, the client and therapist direct the other group participants to reenact the moment, allowing the client a chance to do things differently, say different things, or respond emotionally in a different way.

What the therapist does: The therapist asks the client to put the group members in position to act out a scene from the past. Then the client and therapist direct the group members and client to act out the scene. The therapist encourages the client to have a different reaction to the scene.

Examples:

1076. Okay, now I would like you to pick someone to act out the part of your mother, now of your father, now your sister and brother. Okay, now put them in the right place so that they can begin the scene. How far apart should they be? Who should be looking at whom? Okay, now tell them what they need to be doing to make this real for you.

1077. Your mom and dad are coming closer together. What is it that you would like to hear them say to one another? What would you like to say to them?

1078. It seems as though your aunt is still way over there. You said previously that you wanted her to be closer to the family. Go ahead and invite her in. Tell her you want her to stand here. Now what do you want to hear from her?

1079. You said that at the moment when everyone laughed at you and called you names you went on the offensive and started fighting. Your emotional reaction was anger, right? Now that we are here again, change that emotional reaction of anger to something else. What are you feeling now?

1080. It seems that you are having a similar emotional response as before. I see the tears and the hurt in your face as those two pushed you away. What would you like to be different this time? Go ahead and tell them what you want them to do and say.

AT HOME

Acting "As If"

Approach aligned with: Individual psychology

Purpose: To encourage clients to function in a different way, see the world differently, and find out that they can engage in other behaviors without the world coming down on them.

What the therapist does: For a prescribed period of time, the therapist asks the client to act in ways similar to the type of person he would like to be. The client is encouraged to act like the person they most want to be like.

Examples:

1081. I want you to pick a time during the day tomorrow, and for one hour act as if you had no worries about how others see you.

1082. I want you to arrive at the party late and stay longer than you normally would.

1083. You are to go to the drug store and find something to complain about and then do it just as your brother-in-law would.

1084. I think you should practice being less vocal in groups by acting as if you were a quiet, timid, shy person the next time your work group gets together.

1085. You have mentioned that you want to be more sexy around your husband. I suggest that tonight you act as if you were "more sexy" by doing the things you mentioned previously.

1086. I want you to schedule a time this weekend, for say, one hour, when you will act as if you were that man you said you wanted to be—more affectionate, more sensitive, more talkative.

1087. For practice, you should act as if you did not have to fight back when the other kids pick on you. You can practice being that person you described to me earlier.

1088. Okay, so now you have described the ideal person you want to be. Now for the rest of the session I want you to act as if you were that person.

1089. You might try acting as if you were her . . . if only for a short time.

1090. It might help if you acted as if in this situation. Maybe you should consult with your image of how the ideal person would handle this situation. You said they would not get upset but see it as a situation for new growth. Maybe you should try acting as if those were your true feelings.

Directive

Approach aligned with: Brief therapy

Purpose: To encourage the client or clients to act, think, or feel differently in regard to a specific issue covered in therapy.

What the therapist does: The therapist gives the family an instruction to follow that encourages the family to behave in a different way. Directives can be either direct or indirect. They can be produced and provided by one therapist, co-therapists, or a team of therapists. Directives usually take shape through restraint from change, paradox, or encouraging more of the same.

Examples:

1091. The team believes that your family would benefit from taking a vacation from the problem. So, you are to pick out one hour a day and give yourselves a vacation from the problem. After the hour is up go back to the way you were.

1092. I do not understand how you were able to improve so quickly. I suggest that you should move slowly in making changes during the next few weeks. That way we can better monitor your progress.

1093. The team is split. Half of us think you should go on the family vacation. The other half think that things have gotten so bad in the system that right now is not the best time for a vacation. We have left it up to you to decide. We just don't know.

1094. I think that you should consider what you could do to make him sexually aroused, but do not do it yet. We should talk about it first . . . make sure you are on the right path.

1095. We agree with you that the family is talking much more clearly with one another. We have seen the change. We want to encourage you to do more of the same in the next few weeks.

1096. I have seen many people who have relapsed back into a depressive state for a few days after they improved as much as you. This type of relapse is to be expected.

1097. We, as a team, have decided that we need to accumulate more data on your problem. So we would like you to continue having these spats and arguments, just like normal, over the next few weeks. Just keep a log of what happens, who said what, how it turned out, and why it happened. We will review this data and get a clearer picture for future sessions during the next session.

Door-in-the-Face Technique

Approach aligned with: Family therapy

Purpose: To enlist the client into following a prescription or recommendation.

What the therapist does: The therapist gives the client a seemingly impossible task to perform followed shortly by the recommendation or request that the therapist actually wanted the client to do. This second request is far more reasonable and something that actually can be accomplished by the client.

Examples:

1098. I want you to keep track of every time you have a feeling this week. You are to write it down in this journal and then write a paragraph about it. Then I want you to take the paragraphs at the end of the day and write a day's synopsis from them. If this is too much, I want you to just write about three or four times when you got upset this week in your journal.

1099. You are to allow the boys to argue. If they do it in public, I want you to draw as much attention to them as possible by yelling "come see the fight." When they have finished fighting I want you to have each of them talk about what their experience was like. Then you are to write each of their stories down and then have them review the stories for accuracy. Maybe it would be better if you were to intervene when the boys start arguing like you have been doing. As you said, it is working better.

1100. When you are unable to sleep, you need to get up, drink three glasses of milk, walk around the house for at least one-half hour, and then read out of this book. On second thought, maybe we should see how one glass of milk does to start off.

1101. You and your husband fight a lot. I want you to take a break from each other for at least two weeks. You will have to work out the details of who takes the kids, how the money is handled, and so on. On second thought, maybe you should just try some of the things you mentioned were working and we should see how that goes.

Foot-in-the-Door Technique

Approach aligned with: Family therapy

Purpose: To get the client or clients to agree to follow through with a prescription.

What the therapist does: The therapist gives the client a simple directive to follow and then, once the client is in agreement with the prescription, the therapist asks the client to complete a more difficult task or assignment.

Examples:

1102. I want you to take a minute right now and write down three things you want to focus on in our time together. (once accomplished) Okay, now I want you to write a one-page paper about how these three things connect with one another before next session.

1103. As we have been talking this week, I have been formulating a homework assignment for you. I want you to pick a moment this week when you feel as though you are being overlooked by others and imagine what you would like them to hear that would help them not overlook you. Okay. (once agreed on) After completing this, I want you to find another moment this week with the same conditions, and rather than just think about it, I want you to find someone you feel you can trust and verbalize it to them.

1104. So last week I asked you to think about what you would do to one another to signal that it was safe for the other partner to start the love-making process. You said you did this. Now I want you to not just think about it, but to actually send the signal . . . and if your partner doesn't receive it, keep sending it until they do.

1105. The team has decided that we want each of you to tell the other family members what you want for dinner tonight. Simple enough, right? Okay, once you have done that, you are to work together as a unit to make sure that each person gets what they wanted for dinner.

Paradox

Approach aligned with: Family therapy

Purpose: To have clients who either are resistant to the influence of the therapist or feel that they have absolutely no control over the problem function in a different way.

What the therapist does: The therapist asks the client or clients to do something that seems to be counterproductive to getting better. Usually, paradox takes one of two main directions—either prescribing for the client that they do what they were already going to do (hoping they will resist this and change their behavior) or asking clients to do the opposite of what would normally be asked for in therapy (hoping they will do the opposite).

Examples:

1106. Okay, so as I understand it, you are having trouble getting to sleep each night. I need you to collect some data for me so I want you to actually use this time of not being able to sleep to our benefit. You are to log what you think about and how little sleep you get for the next two weeks. Try to stay on the same pace of the very little sleep you have been getting over the last few months.

1107. As we end this week, I want to have you do something for me. You have mentioned that you seem to have no way of lessening your depression. So, I want to get some more information about your problem. I want you to schedule thirty minutes each day for you to be depressed. This needs to be on a regular basis, and it needs to be for the entire thirty minutes.

1108. As a family, you have a lot of strengths and power. It is clear to us that you really have tried a lot in dealing with this problem. We suggest, however, that sometimes it is not possible to change a problem of this magnitude, but instead we must learn to endure and live with it. In the next few weeks we believe that this is the best course of action.

1109. It seems apparent that this family really likes to argue and bicker. We think this is healthy and would not like you to change this aspect of who you are as a group.

Self-monitoring

Approach aligned with: Cognitive-Behavioral therapy

Purpose: To help the client attain greater insight into a behavior, thought, or feeling through documentation of the event.

What the therapist does: The therapist has the client keep a daily record of their events, actions, behaviors, thoughts, and/or reactions. The client then uses such records to evaluate her behaviors, thoughts, and/or actions.

Examples:

1110. Between this week and next, I want you to keep track of your thoughts in regard to the loss of your mother. To do this, I want you to keep a running journal that indicates a brief description of the thought and the date, time, and place that the thought occurred to you.

1111. I would like for you to take this notebook and keep track of your moments of anger. In this column you will indicate the date and time of the event. In this column you will record what your physical reaction was—for example, red ears, clenched fists, et cetera.

1112. We talked a lot this week about decision making, so, for homework, I want you to write down at least three times in the next week when you have made a decision. You will document what you were thinking, what the alternatives were, how you felt about each of the alternatives, and the outcome of your decision.

1113. The two of you have talked at length about how bad the morning can be at your house. I agree that something needs to change. However, before we decide on what needs to change, we need some data. Every morning, for the next week, you are both to write down observations that you make regarding what happened, who did and said what, and what the general feeling of the morning was that day.

1114. One thing that may help you in your efforts to stop smoking is to first document when you crave a smoke the most. Use a sheet of paper to track the date, time, and place of each smoking fit.

Shame Attack

Approach aligned with: Cognitive-Behavioral therapy

Purpose: To have clients come to understand that they can behave, think, and feel in a different way without the world coming to an end, and that doing things that they once dreaded as being terribly problematic aren't really that bad.

What the therapist does: The therapist gives a homework assignment in which the client is asked to do that which they dread the most. The therapist must make sure that the client is not put into a harmful or nontherapeutic situation.

Examples:

1115. Okay, so you said that you would never show up late to a dinner party, right? And I understand that your mother is throwing one this weekend. I want you to show up fifteen minutes late for her party. Let me know what happens.

1116. You seem to be assured that when people show emotion of any kind in a business meeting they tend to be dismissed. This week at your weekly meeting, I want you to show some type of emotion to at least one person. You decide who and what.

1117. You believe that if you were to go up to someone and say that you found them attractive, they would laugh at you and make fun of you, right? And your notion is that every person on the planet would do that. I want you to test this theory by expressing such feelings to at least four people this week to see what their reactions are.

1118. I heard you say that your mother would crumble if you actually shared that with her. I suspect that there might be some other outcomes. I want you to take a moment when things are calm and do just that.

1119. You said that you are always aware of when others want you to leave. This week, at your book club, stick around at least twenty minutes after the moment you feel people want you to leave. Experience what difference there is, if any, from that time until the time you actually leave.

Stop and Monitor

Approach aligned with: Cognitive-Behavioral therapy

Purpose: To help clients maintain a consistent focus on their thoughts, self-statements, and cognitions.

What the therapist does: The therapist asks the client to either wear or have something in plain sight (a marker) that will help the client remember to stop and write down what they are thinking in that moment. The information the client writes down is then analyzed by both the client and therapist for themes, patterns, growth, and regression.

Examples:

1120. Okay, so you have decided to wear a rubber band around your wrist to remind you that you are to stop and write down what you are thinking.

1121. Remember that every time you look at your TV and see the white piece of paper taped to the front, you are to write down your thoughts.

1122. I hear you saying that you are going to tie a piece of ribbon around your wrist to remind you to log your thoughts. Remember to bring that log with you next week.

1123. As a way of keeping track of when it is time to journal your thoughts and emotions, I want you to document them every time you notice that ring you just moved to your pinky finger.

1124. So wearing something around your ankle like a bracelet will help you remember to journal your thoughts.

1125. It sounds like you have decided to wear a string around your wrist to remind you that you are to stop and write down what you are thinking.

1126. I understand that every time you look at your computer and see the pink Post-it note attached to the side, you are to write down your thoughts.

1127. You said that you listen a lot to the radio. You also said that when you listen, sometimes you get to feeling bad because the station you listen to plays slow love songs. So, I want you to stop and write down exactly what the name of the song is when you find yourself going to that sad place.

Ordeals

Approach aligned with: Family therapy, Individual therapy

Purpose: To get the client(s) to abandon the symptom.

What the therapist does: The therapist gives the client a prescription that is either straightforward or paradoxical. The straightforward ordeal is one in which the therapist asks the client to do something unpleasant but which is good for them because it replaces the symptom. The paradoxical ordeal is one in which the therapist asks the client to perform more of the symptom, which either forces them to recognize they have control over it or stops them from performing the symptom altogether because they choose to resist the therapist.

Examples:

1128. I understand that you are having a lot of difficulty sleeping at night, and that is causing you to miss out on getting all of your reading done. I want you to go to bed each night this week with this task in mind. If you are unable to fall asleep within the first thirty minutes of entering your bed, you are to get up and start reading. You must read for at least four hours.

1129. You have convinced me as a family that this problem takes control and won't let go until it has had its way with you. This can be very difficult. So, this week, I want you to pay homage to the problem, which we are calling "badland." This is what I want you to do. Each of you is to write a three-page letter to the badland outlining the positive effects it has had on your life. Write down what the problem does that makes you feel comfortable. Then when you get together as a family this week, each of you must read the entire letter you wrote to the badland. Finally, you may discuss among one another what ideas you have for limiting its effect.

1130. Okay, so we have talked for a while about how you have great difficulty sleeping at night. This is not such an uncommon problem. But for you it seems to have a strong place in your life. So what I want you to do is agree to try something that will seem rather goofy. When you find yourself awake at night, get up and clean one room in your house. No matter which room you decide on, make sure that you do not go back to sleep before the room is completely clean. And, do not clean the same room twice in a row.

Bibliotherapy

Approach aligned with: Cognitive-Behavioral therapy

Purpose: To provide the client with a specific homework assignment that uses books, articles, audiotapes, or videotapes as a means to learning about a specific issue or topic germane to his therapy.

What the therapist does: The therapist gives a specific prescription of what to read or review by the next session. The therapist may ask the client to focus on a specific area or general concepts.

Examples:

1131. For homework this week I want you to read Glasser's book *Positive Addiction.*

1132. We have talked a lot this week about our sense of feeling as if you would like the world to be different. I would like you to read the book *Ishmael* between now and our next session.

1133. This magazine article talks about the effect of living in a home with a parent who is an alcoholic. I want you to read it before our next session. I want you to focus a lot of attention on the beliefs and messages the author was giving herself when she was your age.

1134. I heard both you and your wife say that you felt as though you would like to have more intimacy in your marriage. I understand you. And I would like both of you to read the book *Radical Presence* before you come back for another session.

1135. We have come a long way in therapy already. I get the feeling that you are ready to start putting some of this stuff we have discussed into motion. I would like you to read a book by Albert Ellis this week called *How to Make Yourself Happy and Remarkably Less Disturbable.* In this book I want you to focus on what control you currently have over your self-messages and self-talk.

1136. Okay, we have talked a lot this week about your wish to get a better sense of how you came to think the way that you do. I want you to read the book *The Earth Is Enough* for next week. Pay close attention to the style the uncles use to train and teach the boy. I will also be interested in talking with you about your reaction to the setting for the book.

Sociogram

Approach aligned with: Universal skill

Purpose: To promote insight into the social world of the client. It is also useful in enabling better use of resources and allies and strengthening connections among and between people.

What the therapist does: The therapist asks the client to develop and draw out her connections with others. The client uses circles to indicate members in a group or clique while lines indicate persons closest with one another. It can be used with families, classes, in work settings, and other groups. It is also useful in this technique to draw in who is rejected or not aligned.

Examples:

1137. So now I want you to put down on paper some of the things we have talked about. I want you to draw a diagram of how your employees function together. Use circles around small groups or pods and connect people by using lines to show those who are closest to one another.

1138. You have a very large extended family. It might help us if we were to plot out how people function with one another in the larger group. Draw an inner circle that represents the core group of your family, followed by outside circles for other subgroups of the family. In situations where family members from differing pods align with one another, draw a line connecting them.

1139. So as I hear you talking you are giving me a lot of details about who is in which group and who likes or dislikes other people. Let's take a few minutes and draw out what you are talking about. Use circles to show cliques and use lines to connect people who are friendly with one another and use arrows to show people who don't get along.

1140. You have shared how there are different groups who align more strongly with one another within your organization. You also said that there are several people who seem to be able to bridge the gap between the groups. I want you to draw this out for a homework assignment this week. Use circles to indicate the different groups and use lines that are connected to show those people who bridge the gaps. Use arrows to show where there are people who tend to reject certain members of the other groups.

Homework

Approach aligned with: Universal skill

Purpose: To maintain contact with the client, keep them focused on therapeutic material, and have them complete an assignment that will promote further growth and development.

What the therapist does: The therapist gives the client a homework assignment to work on and complete before returning to therapy the next session. Homework assignments can range from direct prescriptions for change—for example, practicing new skills—to paradoxical prescriptions—for example, prescribing a relapse.

Examples:

1141. I want you to work on something before we meet again. I want you to keep a list of all the times when your husband does something sweet and thoughtful for you or anyone else.

1142. You are to go home and practice being assertive. I want you to first be assertive with your family members, and then when you have the courage, try being assertive with someone from work.

1143. You need to keep a journal of the times Johnny wets the bed between now and next session.

1144. It sounds like you have a lot of trouble getting to school on time. I want you to keep a daily log of the foods you eat after 7:00 PM.

1145. The team believes that you have really changed a lot this last week. We want you to do nothing in regard to changing before next session.

1146. The next time that you begin to fight you need to prolong it to at least an hour. That way you will be able to give a much better, blow-by-blow description of your different fighting styles when we meet next week.

1147. Between now and the next time we meet I want you to practice meeting people. You are to introduce yourself to at least one person each day.

1148. Your homework assignment this week is to find out how many members of your extended family believe, as you do, that having a mental illness is a necessary part of being included in the family system.

CHAPTER 12

Abandoned Mine Shaft

Mines serve an important purpose. Valuable minerals, raw materials, gems, and rare metals are extracted from them. In the past, when the mines were spent of their value, companies would often abandon them, leaving an open shaft. Similarly, the skills found in this section leave deep shafts which, once entered, are difficult to back away from. For example, even if advice a therapist freely doles out to his clients sometimes "works" (even a blind pig gets an occasional acorn), the therapist may be doing a tremendous disservice to both the client and the profession of therapy by giving advice. If the client now assumes that therapists exist to tell him how to live his life, what is best for him, and what decisions he should make, the client may well assume a dependency role, wrongly concluding that therapists will relieve him of having to make his own decisions in life. This is not the true role of the therapist, of course. School does not provide therapists with answers to the problems their clients will face. Both you and your clients need to recognize that fact. Therapists are advised to avoid as much as possible the "skills" located in this chapter.

Social Greeting

Approach aligned with: Skill to avoid

Purpose: To greet the client in a way she might expect to be greeted in a normal conversation. There is no real value to it other than providing a start to the session—a start to the talking. Social greetings are also used to end conversations as well.

What the therapist does: The therapist, lacking a specific way of starting the session, begins the session by talking as if it is a normal daily discussion.

Note: Though seen as some therapists as being a problematic way to start a session, in some instances, depending on local customs, needs of the particular client, and/or therapeutic approach of the clinician, starting and ending a session with a social greeting may be considered to have therapeutic value.

Examples:

1149. Hello.

1150. Hey.

1151. It's nice to see you.

1152. Greetings.

1153. Nice to meet you.

1154. Welcome back.

1155. Good afternoon.

1156. How about that weather.

1157. See you later.

1158. Good-bye.

1159. What's up.

1160. Hey, good to see you.

1161. Nice to see you again.

1162. Nice weather out there, huh?

1163. Wow, that's a nice purse.

1164. Man, I've had a busy day.

1165. Hot out there?

1166. Did you find parking okay?

1167. Good to see you.

1168. Is it still raining out there?

Advice Giving

Approach aligned with: Skill to avoid

Purpose: To provide the client with what the therapist believes is the right answer. If used as a primary therapy technique, it encourages the client to rely on the therapist or others for answers. It detracts from the helping relationship as a mutual connection and makes it a one-up, one-down interaction, with the client being in the one-down position.

What the therapist does: The therapist provides the client with advice that she thinks the client should follow to have a better life. This advice may take the form of a direct comment or subtle, below-the-surface comments.

Examples:

1169. You should date that other guy.

1170. It might be wise for you to leave your current relationship.

1171. Your family has no right to pressure you like that—you should put them in their place.

1172. If you want to know my opinion, I believe that no one has the right to treat you that way.

1173. You should learn how to handle your anger better. It will help you in the future.

1174. You might want to rethink going out with her. She sounds like she may be more trouble than she's worth.

1175. In my life, I have found it important to tell others how I feel about things. You should learn to do the same.

1176. I hear you. Your family does not really respect all that you do for them. You should just leave them for a while and they will then understand how important you really are.

1177. It is important that you develop a thicker skin. You should not let things like what your mom said bother you.

1178. You should really try meeting other people. It would do you a lot of good.

1179. I don't think I would try to do that.

1180. I believe that things will work out if you stop focusing on the negative side of things and start looking at the brighter side of life.

Band-Aiding

Approach aligned with: Skill to avoid

Purpose: To save the client from experiencing pain or trouble in his life.

What the therapist does: The therapist jumps in and saves the client from experiencing strong emotional feelings by strongly communicating to the client that everything will be fine and work out in the end.

Examples:

1181. Hey, don't cry, you know that this is only temporary.

1182. I know you said that you lost your marriage of twenty-four years, but everything will be okay. I know lots of people in worse situations that turned out fine.

1183. We have been talking about losing your mother and father, and I must share that when I lost my parents, it was hard for a while. But I got over and through it. You will too.

1184. You know, what makes us upset and hurt, makes us stronger. Let's focus only on the good because in the end, you know, things always work out all right.

1185. There, there, things will be okay. Let's talk about something else.

1186. Hey, don't worry. I can help you figure out all of this. It will be all right. Don't worry.

1187. Okay, so what I think we need to do is back off a bit and focus on other stuff. You are getting too upset right now. We can go back later.

1188. You really seem upset by this. Maybe we should focus on other stuff right now.

1189. I think it is time to discuss your thoughts on the matter—right now it is too emotional for you.

1190. I am sorry that we have talked about this today. It really seems to upset you, and I don't think that is what you need.

1191. Maybe we should not focus on the problem for a while. It seems as though you get sad when we address it.

1192. Things will be all right if you just let them work themselves out.

1193. I think that your problem will go away in time, so don't worry so much about it. Trust me, I know that things look bad now, but in time you will heal, and you will look back on this and laugh.

Condemning Questions

Approach aligned with: Skill to avoid

Purpose: To limit the client's self-expression or desire to openly discuss her problem. To covertly get the client to change her mind on an issue.

What the therapist does: The therapist asks questions that have the effect of putting the client down for what she is expressing or feeling and/or make the client feel as though she is being judged and is wrong for expressing views.

Examples:

1194. Are you sure that you feel that way?

1195. Do you think that is right?

1196. Are you sure that you want to say that?

1197. Don't you want some time to rethink that?

1198. Would you like to rethink that response?

1199. Are you sure about that?

1200. Perhaps you are not really feeling that way—are you?

1201. Is that your real thought about the matter?

1202. Can you think about why what you said might be wrong?

1203. Don't you think that goes against what is right?

1204. Don't you think you are being too hard on her for what she did?

1205. Have you considered being nicer to her when she acts like that?

1206. Do you really believe that is the right thing to do?

1207. Have you considered the possibility, and I am just thinking out loud here, but have you considered that you should be less judgmental of others?

1208. What would life be like if you were more forgiving of others?

1209. Why is it that you never want to do what your husband wants?

1210. How can it be that you never call your mother, even on her birthday?

Dis-identification

Approach aligned with: Skill to avoid

Purpose: This is the sign of a therapist who has become emotionally isolated from or removed from the client.

What the therapist does: The therapist loses the ability to understand the deeper meaning of the client or hear the voice and story of the client.

Examples: *To the client:*

1211. I am not sure what the real problem is.

1212. So what is upsetting you about that?

1213. You sound upset, but I really don't understand why.

1214. Maybe we should talk about something else.

1215. I'm not really following you right now. What did you say?

1216. How does that make you feel? Angry? Happy?

1217. Why do you keep talking about that?

1218. Is there something meaningful in that?

1219. No, I am not bored. I'm listening.

1220. I am trying to follow you.

1221. So what's the problem?

To self:

1222. I have worked with people like this; this really isn't a problem.

1223. I have overcome much more difficult things than this; this client should just buck up and deal with life.

1224. Just get over it.

1225. What is the big deal? Just deal with it.

1226. Really, this person thinks they need therapy because they are upset with their husband about his hygiene?

Minimization

Approach aligned with: Skill to avoid

Purpose: To make the therapist more comfortable with the conversation by implying that what the client is talking about is less significant, important, powerful, or real than it really is to the client.

What the therapist does: The therapist provides clear direction to the client that what he is feeling or thinking is less important than it really is. The therapist promotes the notion that the client is making it out to be bigger than it really is. The client is left with the feeling that his thoughts or feelings are not as important or true to life as he might want or expect them to be.

Examples:

1227. You really don't feel that bad do you?

1228. How is it that you can be so happy about that? It really wasn't that big of a deal.

1229. It seems as though you make everything out to be something bigger than it really is.

1230. I don't think that what we have done in these sessions has been all that good.

1231. I have had several patients who suffered from the same ailments as you. They worked a lot harder and got better much quicker.

1232. You're not really upset by that are you?

1233. How can you let something like that make you mad. Are you really all that mad?

1234. You may be making a bigger deal out of this than is necessary.

1235. I would be careful acting so happy about this. It isn't that important.

1236. I really don't see what is useful in this for you.

1237. You said you felt angry, but you were really just upset, right?

1238. By "life changing" you mean somewhat important.

Adding the following words before a reflection of feeling when not warranted:

1239. Kinda

1240. Sort of

1241. A little

1242. Somewhat

Over-identification

Approach aligned with: Skill to avoid

Purpose: This is when the therapist becomes so emotionally involved in the client or clients that she loses objectivity. This is a form of countertransference.

What the therapist does: The therapist makes statements that disclose personal issues in a way that is nontherapeutic for the client and that refocus the session on the therapist and her needs.

Examples: *To client:*

1243. I am terribly saddened by the fact that you are having trouble with this.

1244. I really wish that I could say or do something, anything that would make things a little better.

1245. I couldn't sleep well this week because I have been thinking about you and your dilemma.

1246. I'm sorry that I am crying but it really makes me sad when you talk like that.

1247. I am hearing your family talk and can't help but go back to a place in my own life when my family talked in a similar way. I am sorry that I can't be of much help right now.

1248. Johnny, you are really being rough with Susan right now. It bothers me to see you talk to her that way.

1249. I can really feel what you are talking about. It reminds me of some stuff from my past. I don't like it when people treat me that way either.

1250. You sound just like my father with all of his negativity and pessimism.

1251. It is hard for me to continue to work with you because of my own stuff. When I look at you and hear you talking about your past, I can't help but go back to a time when I, too, was involved in drugs and alcohol. It is hard to separate myself from you in those moments.

1252. Your pain is my pain.

To self:

1253. Man, this is terrible, I can't get that client out of my mind.

1254. Maybe if we figure out what's wrong it will help me in my own life.

1255. It is really hard to hear her talk about her mom. I am just the same way.

Double Questions

Approach aligned with: Skill to avoid

Purpose: To confuse the client by asking two or more questions, thereby limiting the client's ability to respond.

What the therapist does: The therapist asks several questions at once that may or may not be connected to one another. This is done in succession so that there is no time for the client to respond to the first question before the second or third question is asked.

Examples:

1256. What were things like for you last week? Did you get a chance to talk to your friend about that situation?

1257. I was curious, how many people know about this issue? And I also wanted to ask you whether or not you had already told your principal about it?

1258. Oh yeah, by the way, how is your sister doing? Is she still recovering from the surgery? Did everything go as expected?

1259. As we have worked together for some time now, I am curious what has worked best for you? What have you discovered about yourself that you did not already know?

1260. How many times a week does this occur? Have you ever tried anything to do it more often?

1261. If you were to start coming to school more often what effect would that have on your grades? How might other people respond to you differently?

1262. What's going on at home this week? How have things changed since the last time we saw each other?

1263. On a scale from one to ten—ten being the best, how is your day going? Are you having a good day?

1264. Why would she do that to you? Did anyone else know about this?

1265. What caused you to think that he didn't like you? Are you going to talk with him again?

1266. I heard you say things are better. What changed to make them better? Are you worried they will go back to the way they were?

1267. When you were talking about that situation, I was wondering why you did that? How did you feel about her saying that to you?

CHAPTER 13

....

Comprehensive Transcript

The following fictional transcript was created to show how a therapist might use the techniques described in this book. The imaginary client is a forty-five-year-old female, recently divorced, with two children (ages twelve and eight). Her presenting problem is that she and the kids are having difficulty adjusting to their new lives. The therapist has a private practice. She has been a therapist for fifteen years.

Several things should be noted regarding this transcript. We used the skills presented in this book in sequence. This was done to demonstrate how to move from rapport building and hearing the client's story (skills found in Chapter 3, The Reflecting Pool) to encouraging the client to do something different (skills found in Chapter 11, Waves in

Motion). In reality, of course, a therapist would not use all of these skills in one session. Further, this session transcript is quite lengthy, again due to adding in all of the skills.

Also note that the therapist spent a lot of time asking questions (Chapter 4, The Questioning Tree). In our own practice we have found that asking a lot of questions can be detrimental to both the rapport with the client and the therapeutic value of the session.

As with any session, real or fictional, there are a multitude of different approaches a therapist might take. This session utilizes various skills and theory bases as the client and therapist move from a superficial to a deeper therapeutic discussion.

Th = Therapist
Cl = Client

1268. Th: Okay, so if I recall our phone conversation, you are worried about how your kids are handling the adjustment to the divorce. And I recall that you said you are having some difficulty as well. (Summary)

Cl: Yeah, I just don't know how to handle all of the stress and problems that come along with being a single mom.

1269. Th: Mhmm. (Minimal Encourager)

Cl: It's like I sometimes think that things would have been better if I had just stayed with the marriage.

1270. Th: You question whether it would have been better to stay married. (Paraphrase)

Cl: Exactly, I mean, maybe we had some troubles, but, overall, it was not the worst thing I ever had to go through. I don't know, I guess I gave up on it rather quickly.

1271. Th: You feel sad that the marriage ended. (Reflection of Feeling)

Cl: Yes, I feel like we could have tried something else.

1272. Th: You believe that you should have been able to fix the marriage. (Reflection of Meaning)

Cl: I know that sounds silly. I mean we tried to stay together for two and a half years. We tried everything, but nothing seemed to work. It really wore me out.

1273. Th: It sounds like you are tired from all of that work. (Reflection of Feeling)

Cl: I always thought that our marriage would last forever.

1274. Th: So what does that say about you that your marriage did not last? (Downward Arrow)

Cl: Well, I guess it says that I failed.

1275. Th: And, so, then what does it say about you that you failed? (Downward Arrow)

Cl: I suspect it means that I am a failure.

1276. Th: So, then, if I hear what you are saying, you believe that people who have marriages that end in divorce are failures. (Downward Arrow)

Cl: Humm. I guess that sounds pretty harsh, doesn't it?

1277. Th: Harsh. (Accent)

Cl: Well, I guess your point is that maybe I am not a complete failure and that a lot of good people have marriages that end in divorce.

1278. Th: Good people have marriages that end in divorce. (Accent)

Cl: Well, yeah, of course, I mean I know a lot of people from my self-help group who are really nice, and work really hard and just had things end in their marriages.

1279. Th: It sounds like you are looking more closely at your belief about what constitutes failing in life. (Summary)

Cl: I am really feeling good about being able to talk to someone about all of this.

1280. Th: I get the sense that carrying the load of weight that you have for so long has really been incredibly difficult. (Empathy)

Cl: Oh my yes. At times I have felt as if I were going to crumble under the weight.

1281. Th: Tell me more about the feeling of crumbling. (Prompt)

[Client and therapist are interrupted by the client's two children, Johnny and Susie.]

1282. Th: Well, I see that you two would like to join us.

Cl: You two can play over there—but don't interrupt.

1283. Th: (to Johnny) You are really working hard to fill that dump truck with sand. (Child's Content of Play)

1284. Th: (to Susie) You are happy to see that the puzzle pieces all fit together. (Child's Feelings)

1285. Th: (to Johnny) You are frustrated by the sand not staying in the dump truck. (Child's Feelings)

1286. Th: (to Susie) You are working hard at building with the blocks. (Child's Content of Play)

[The children move back outside to play in the other room.]

1287. Th: (to mom) Do your children always play so well alongside one another? (Closed Question)

Cl: Yes.

1288. Th: How did you raise these children so well while working so hard on your marriage? (Open Question)

Cl: Oh, well, we both, my husband and I, we decided that it was really important to make sure the kids didn't get run over by our problems. We tried very hard to keep our troubles away from them as much as possible.

1289. Th: Okay, let me check this out with you. Do I have it right that amidst your worst nightmare, a marriage that is going bad, you and your husband focused a lot of time and energy on making sure the kids were okay? (Checkout)

Cl: Yeah, I guess that's right.

1290. Th: Okay, so let's recap our discussion so far. We have talked about your feelings of failing in the marriage, your wonderful kids and how protective you were of them, and the heavy weight you are carrying with the loss of the marriage. (Summary) Did I miss anything? (Closed Question)

Cl: No, I think that covers it pretty well.

1291. Th: Okay, then, tell, me, what would be different in your life if you were not carrying this heavy weight? (Asking the Question)

Cl: Oh my. I can't even think. Well I guess I would be happier, and I would probably get out of the house more and have more energy to do more things.

1292. Th: So, if I hear you right, you are saying that carrying this weight keeps you from doing things that you might otherwise like to do? (Checkout)

Cl: Yeah, but it's like, well, I guess the logic I use is that no one really wants to be around me, you know with the divorce and all, but they are just being nice, you know, taking care of the poor single mom.

1293. Th: What proof do you have to this theory that the only reason people would like to be around you is that they want to do a good deed? (Cognitive Disputation)

Cl: I don't know, I just always thought that way about people who had just had a divorce, like I felt bad for them or something.

1294. Th: Do the kids receive the same treatment from others, where other people feel bad for them? (Closed Question)

Cl: Sometimes, yes. I think that there are teachers and parents who say things like "it must be really tough to have to go through that." But I guess people think that more about me.

1295. Th: Oh, okay, then, I want to know what effect it has on your children when you become aware that someone is doing something nice for you just because you are the "poor divorced mom"? (Circular Questioning)

Cl: I think I notice that the most when I get quiet and then the kids just sit around watching me and there is a mood that takes over in the house. It is like a mood of feeling like sad and lonely at the same time.

1296. Th: This mood thing that you described. I'm going to ask you a very strange question about it, but I want to get a better picture in my head of what it looks and feels like. Can you tell me what color it is? (Externalizing the Problem)

Cl: I never thought of it having a color . . . I see it as being dark purple with dark red streaks along its side.

1297. Th: Oh, I can start to see it. Tell me what shape it is. (Externalizing the Problem)

Cl: I think it's like a blob that changes shape. But mostly it is round, or maybe kind of like an oval shape.

1298. Th: Oh yeah, I can see it. Now for a really strange question. Does it change size or just stay the same? (Externalizing the Problem)

Cl: It gets smaller sometimes.

1299. Th: Right, I can imagine it as you have described it. So, I wonder, if you and the kids went to bed tonight, and something magical happened, unknown to you, and the purplish, red-striped, oval blob suddenly disappeared from your life, what would be the first thing to let you know it had completely gone away? (Miracle Question)

Cl: I don't know. That's a hard question to answer . . . I guess that the first thing would be that we would feel lighter and it wouldn't be as dark.

1300. Th: What one word or phrase would you use to describe how you would feel about being free from the grip of the blob? (Probe)

Cl: I would have to say liberated!

1301. Th: And your kids would answer? (Probe)

Cl: They would agree with liberated, but I think they would say happy!

1302. Th: So, which would you like to focus on together, working on defeating the blob or trying to figure out why your marriage ended in a divorce? (Forced Choice Question)

Cl: I definitely would rather focus on defeating the blob.

1303. Th: Okay, so up to this point we have discussed several important issues. You have described the heavy weight of feeling like a failure for your divorce, we have talked about how your children were protected by you and your former husband as much as possible, and we have gotten a clearer picture of the blob that is in your life right now. (Summary)

Cl: Yeah, and I feel like if I can get this blob destroyed, things will really be in a much better place.

1304. Th: So, if I hear you right, you are saying that you have a lot more hope right now than when you came in, is that right? (Checkout)

Cl: Yes, absolutely.

1305. Th: Then I have a terrible question to ask. What would cause you to go backwards and feel as if there is less hope for the situation? (The Terrible Question)

Cl: Nothing I can think of. I really think I see the light at the end of the tunnel.

1306. Th: Okay, then let's shift gears for a second and I want to ask you a little about your children. Can you tell me what you believe they are doing right now? I mean, obviously they are outside playing, but what is really happening between them? (Triadic Questioning)

Cl: I think they are playing together like always, and you know, they seem to get along so well together. I suspect they are cooperating and talking and developing a close bond with one another.

1307. Th: So, which one of them would be the first to notice how much hope you have right now for things to get better? (Circular Questioning)

Cl: Definitely Johnny. He is very aware of my mood. Susie is less apt to pay attention to how I am feeling.

1308. Th: Let's stick with that theme of hope for a minute. On a scale from one to ten, ten being the most hope possible. Where are you and your children in terms of having hope for things to get better? (Scaling Question)

Cl: I am at an eight, Johnny would be at a six, and Susie would be at a nine.

1309. **Th:** Wow, that seems like a lot of hope you guys have. So what is it that Susie knows about the situation that you and Johnny have not discovered yet? (Circular Questioning)

Cl: I don't really know. I guess she lives her life paying a lot more attention to the good stuff. She never seems to let things bother her for too long.

[Children enter the room again.]

1310. **Th:** Wow, as if right on cue. We were just talking about having hope for you all to get to feeling better. Mom, did you want to tell them what you were saying? (Closed Question)

Cl: Well, I guess. We were discussing how things can get kind of down at home, and that maybe that will change in the future. And I said that I thought both of you had a lot of hope that things would get turned around for us.

1311. **Th:** Johnny, what did you hear your mom say just then? (Communication Clarification)

Johnny: She said that she thinks things will get better.

[Children grab some toys and leave the room.]

Cl: So what should I do to make things better?

1312. **Th:** Well, I would like to give you a magic answer, but I believe that you will have to discover what works best for you. As we talked about on the phone, in this process, I can't give you advice on how to lead your life. (Structuring)

Cl: I knew you were going to say something like that.

1313. **Th:** Well, we've certainly covered a lot of ground up to this point. I'm wondering what you are experiencing right now? (Here and Now)

Cl: I feel like I am being heard and I feel like a weight is being lifted off of me.

1314. **Th:** For me, I think that we have gotten to know each other, developed some rapport, and have discussed some important things for you, and it seems as though we started talking about feelings you have that are on the surface and then made our way down to some of your core beliefs. (Process Illumination)

Cl: Yeah, and I realized that I don't usually talk that much about most of this stuff. It feels good to do this.

1315. **Th:** I'm glad to hear that this is a good experience for you. In my experience, I have found that some clients need a lot of time to trust me enough to share, while others feel safe and secure very quickly. (Technical Expert)

Cl: I can see that. There have been some times when I was afraid of what you might say or think when I said something. I felt like it might sound stupid.

1316. Th: It makes me feel a bit sad that you feel as though some of your thoughts and experiences might be stupid, or at least sound stupid. (Model-Setting Participant)

Cl: Wow, I'm feeling a bit nervous right now.

1317. Th: Okay, let's take a minute or two and discuss what just happened here. I think you are feeling like you are on a hot seat right now. (Blocking)

Cl: Yeah, I think it is interesting to think that someone cares about how I feel. I mean, are you really sad—or is that just something therapists say?

1318. Th: Well first, I am sad about that. (Self-disclosure) But, it sounds like you have a direct statement behind that question. Can we try to figure out what you were trying to say to me with your question? (Changing Questions to Statements)

Cl: Okay.

1319. Th: I suspect that what you were really saying is that you are not sure whether I am being open and honest with you about how I am feeling. (Interpretation)

Cl: Okay, I can see that.

1320. Th: So I want you to come up with a statement that captures how you feel and what you are thinking, rather than asking me a question. (Changing Questions to Statements)

Cl: Okay, that's going to be hard. Let's see.

1321. Th: Try starting with "I feel" or "I think." (Changing Questions to Statements)

Cl: Okay. I feel that sometimes you are being honest and like a real person, but other times you are saying things just like a therapist would say.

1322. Th: Okay, I understand you. And what I want you to hear from my perspective is that the purpose of our meeting is to help you work through some issues. In that process, I will use a number of different techniques and styles. And I understand that at times it may feel more like therapy, and other times may feel more like we are friends, but our main purpose is to help you cope with your divorce. (Clarifying the Purpose)

Cl: (starts crying) This is all a lot to deal with right now. I have a lot of feelings that are just ready to explode. (crying even more) I just want things to be good again.

1323. Th: I can really see the pain you are in. (Reflection of Feeling) I want you to think for a minute about something. And, we can take all of the time you need. But think for a while about what two or three things you want to know in a different way when we are done here today. (Capping)

Cl: Umm, okay. Well. There's really only one. I want to know how to stop blaming myself for the divorce.

1324. Th: Okay, so the main issue is the sense of guilt you feel over the divorce? (Defining the Problem/Issue)

Cl: Oh my, yeah!

1325. Th: Okay, so then, if things work out for us this session, and it goes really well, and you start feeling less guilty, what will be different? (Defining Goals/Objectives/Outcomes)

Cl: I don't know. I guess I'll feel like I felt earlier today—lighter somehow.

1326. Th: Okay, so then one of our goals is for you to learn to give yourself permission to go to that place where you feel lighter more often? (Defining Goals/Objectives/Outcomes)

Cl: Yeah, that would be nice!

1327. Th: So, if I am catching your story right, you have blamed yourself a lot for the divorce, which means that you took on the burden, or most of the burden, for both you and your husband. And now, while still carrying this burden or responsibility for the entire thing, you are trying to help your kids get through this. That really is a lot of weight to carry. You must be really strong to do this. (Reframe)

Cl: Geez. I never thought of it in that way. No wonder I am so tired all the time.

1328. Th: Right. So how can your strength be of better use? (Exploring Alternatives)

Cl: I don't know. I guess I could use my strength to be happier. Is that what you mean?

1329. Th: Well sure, that's one way. What I was asking you about is how you can build on this strength you have of being able to handle so much while still thinking of others. (Identifying/Building Strengths)

Cl: I guess I could be more carefree and let things go and not worry about them as much. That might help me use my strength in other ways.

1330. Th: Oh, I see, so you and Susie would be more alike in this way . . .a carefree attitude toward life? (Linking)

Cl: Yeah, I could use a little more of that in my life.

1331. Th: I must share with you that I am so impressed by not only how well your kids are learning from you, but how you honor them by learning from them as well. Your family is very impressive in that way. (Compliment)

Cl: Thank you. My husband and I always tried to be good parents, and we thought that our kids were teaching us as much about life as we were teaching them.

1332. Th: Yeah, that seems about right for what you have described. I am curious as to what other things you might be able to use as ways of dealing with this that your children are currently using? (Exploration)

Cl: Hmmm. Let's see. I like the carefree one. That's good. Oh . . . I guess I could . . .well . . .now . . .let's see . . .I like how Johnny just lets things roll off his back. He doesn't seem to carry them around as much as I do. But, I don't know, I am the mom, it's my job to worry, right?

1333. Th: So one of your rules in life is that moms are supposed to worry. I wonder if there is an exception to that rule? (Focus on Exceptions)

Cl: Well I don't know. I guess that's just how I am.

1334. Th: Is it possible that you carry all of this heavy weight so others will see how strong you really are? (Interpretation)

Cl: Wow. That doesn't sound good does it?

1335. Th: Well, I guess I see this picture of you in my head. And it is probably not what you would want to hear. But, I see you as a locomotive engine pulling a train up a hill. (Metaphor)

Cl: Yeah, and my job, my kids, my divorce, all of it. I'm pulling all of it up the hill.

1336. Th: Yeah, right, and once you get to the top of the hill, it will be all of that weight that will give you enough momentum to go the rest of the way without having such a terrible struggle up another hill. (Redefining)

Cl: Wow, that really sounds nice. I would like that.

1337. Th: I want to go back for a moment, however, and pick on some things you said. On the one hand, you said that you don't like carrying the weight and burden of the divorce. And you also said that people notice you as the "poor single mom." I wonder if you don't get something from being seen as the "poor single mom" that makes it hard to put down the extra weight. (Confrontation and Spitting in the Client's Soup)

Cl: No. No. I really don't like being seen in that way.

1338. Th: As I watched you say that, I saw you start to wring your hands and look down at your feet. That is the first time I saw you react in that way. (Observation)

Cl: Well. I don't like the idea of wanting to be seen as the poor single mom. That bothers me a lot.

1339. Th: I notice that you are slumping in your chair as if a weight was just put on your back. (Confirmation)

Cl: Yeah. I kinda feel that way right now.

1340. Th: Okay. Obviously we are not doing something that is helpful to you right now. In fact it seems like we are causing the situation to worsen. Let's shift gears and try another angle, okay? (Cutting Off)

Cl: That would be good.

1341. Th: Yeah, and I am aware that you are working really hard to not feel so slumped over in life. (Affirmation)

Cl: Yes. That is a good way to put it, I do feel slumped over most of the time.

1342. Th: And as you say that, I see you lifting your body up a little bit, and that gives me the impression that you are feeling stronger right now. (Providing Feedback)

Cl: Yeah I am. I feel a little lighter than a few minutes ago. I guess I didn't realize how much I say with my body though. It is strange to have someone watching and analyzing every move that you make.

1343. Th: As you say that I feel as if maybe I am focusing too much on your body language and that what I am sharing with you about what I am seeing is not helping us work effectively on the problem. (Immediacy)

Cl: Yeah, I agree.

1344. Th: In therapy, there are times when we have to stop and reflect on what we are doing to make sure that we are making the most effective use of our time together. We will do this several times over the course of our sessions. (Providing Information)

Cl: Okay, so that's to make sure we don't get going in a wrong direction for too long, right?

[Children enter the room.]

1345. Th: I have a daughter, she is a little younger than yours, she's just turned three. (Self-disclosure and Providing Information)

Cl: Oh, that's a fun age. Well, I think all of the ages are fun.

1346. Th: (leaning over to play with the children) I am happy to be playing with you right now. (Therapist's Feelings)

1347. Th: I am playing with the doll. (Therapist's Content of Play)

[After several more minutes of play, the children leave once again.]

Cl: I really love my kids. They are the world to me. You know, watching you play alongside of them, I can imagine you are a really good parent. You just seem to naturally know what to do, and with all that you know about psychological stuff, I bet your daughter will turn out great.

1348. Th: Thank you, but I want to go back and pick up a piece of what you said. You said that your children are the world to you. (Holding the Focus)

Cl: Yeah, I did say that. Hmm. I just can't imagine not having them around. They are so precious.

[Children reenter the room.]

1349. Th: Hi again. You know, Johnny. You looked at your mom as if you had something to say. Did you want to say something to her? (Drawing Out)

Johnny: Mom, when are you going to be done?

Cl: Well, pretty soon. Why don't you go back out and play.

Johnny: I want to go home now.

Cl: We are going to be done soon. You can handle playing for a little bit longer.

Johnny: But we've been here forever.

[Johnny and Susie tell their mother what they think of her keeping them here, and that she was the cause of the divorce. Mom begins to show real distress and pain on her face as the children state their case.]

1350. Th: Okay, let's give mom a minute to regroup. I think you have both given her a lot to think about right now. (Protection)

1351. Th: Wow. I am amazed at how calmly you handled yourself in that situation. (Joining)

Cl: That happens sometimes.

1352. Th: That must be hard to be at the mercy of your children as they blame you for something that you already blame yourself for. It must really add even more to your already heavy load. (Unbalancing)

Cl: You can't imagine how bad that hurts sometimes.

1353. Th: (to the children) I heard you both saying things that lead me to believe that you are really mad about what has happened. I want you to tell me, if you can think of any examples, of how your mom is different in a good way since your parents split up. (Shifting the Focus)

Johnny: (after thinking for a while) I like how she plays more with us.

Susie. Yeah, and she doesn't yell as much.

1354. Th: You both seem to have some positive things to say about your mom. But I understand that sometimes you get really mad at her. This hasn't been an easy situation for any of you. (Summary)

1355. Th: (to mom) I want you to take a moment and imagine that we had a camera in here. What would a snapshot of this moment look like? (Camera Check)

Cl: If the camera were over there, it would be a picture of children playing and two adults talking. Everyone would be hard at work and with serious looks on their faces. There would also be a dark cloud hanging over the whole picture.

1356. Th: Okay. So now I want to try to move our session in another direction. I want you to close your eyes and go to a place that is warm and safe. Imagine that place that you like to go in your mind where you are at peace. (Creative Imagery)

Cl: Okay.

1357. Th: Now I want you to imagine what we had talked about earlier. I want you to see yourself being more carefree. (Focused Imagery)

Cl: Oh my. All right.

1358. Th: Okay. Now that you have seen a picture with a dark cloud and imagined yourself being more carefree, I want to know what the positive aspects to allowing yourself to make this change would be. (Logical Consequences)

Cl: I would feel freer, more relaxed, I wouldn't feel like I was always under pressure and worn out. I would be my old self.

1359. Th: Okay, then what would the cons be to doing this?

Cl: I would have to find someone or something else to blame for the divorce. And I would be afraid that the cloud would come back.

1360. Th: Okay, you said that you would feel more relaxed. So I want to try a relaxation exercise with you. Now get into a relaxed position with nothing on your body crossed . . .

uncross your legs . . . fingers . . . arms . . . now focus on your breathing . . . pay attention to the air going in . . . the air going out . . . get complete control of your breathing . . . breathe in . . . now breathe out . . . now focus on your toes . . . feel the tension in your toes . . . now make your toes tight and hard and firm . . . now relax your toes, make them soft and warm and relaxed . . . now make your toes tight and hard and firm . . . now relax your toes, make them soft and warm and relaxed . . . now move to your feet . . . feel the tension in your feet. Now make your feet tight and hard and firm . . . now relax your feet, make them soft and warm and relaxed . . . now make your feet tight and hard and firm . . . now relax your feet, make them soft and warm and relaxed . . . focus on your breathing and feel the air going in and out, with each breath you are feeling more relaxed and calm . . . now focus on your calves. Feel the tension in your calves . . . now make your calves tight and hard and firm . . . now relax your calves, make them soft and warm and relaxed . . . now make your calves tight and hard and firm . . . now relax your calves, make them soft and warm and relaxed . . . okay, now focus on your thighs . . . feel the tension in your thighs. Make your thighs tight and hard and firm . . . now relax your thighs, make them soft and warm and relaxed . . . make your thighs tight and hard and firm . . . now relax your thighs, make them soft and warm and relaxed . . . now focus on your hips . . . feel the tension in your hips . . . now make your hips tight and hard and firm . . . now relax your hips, make them soft and warm and relaxed . . . now make your hips tight and hard and firm . . . now relax your hips, make them soft and warm . . . . (Progressive Relaxation) (*Note:* This procedure is followed for the rest of the body.)

Cl: Wow. That was relaxing. That was great!

1361. Th: Okay. So now that you are relaxed, I want you to take a minute and think about something. Imagine that I want you to imagine yourself defeating the thoughts that want to make you feel tense and burdened. Right now, imagine yourself doing just that. (Imaginal Treatment)

Cl: Okay. Wow, I can feel myself staying relaxed and calm. I feel like the entire weight is gone right now.

1362. Th: (turning to the children) I wonder if you can grab those crayons over there and the paper so we can make a picture. Okay fine. I want each of you—mom you are included as well—each of you to draw a picture of your family as you see it. (Conjoint Family Drawing)

[Mom and children work on pictures.]

1363. Th: Okay, that's fine. Now, what do you see in common in all of these pictures?

Johnny: Dad is in all of them.

Cl: Wow. I didn't even realize that. What does that mean?

Susie: I miss him.

1364. Th: Mom, I see you hunching over a bit right now. I want to challenge you to use the skills we practiced earlier to defeat the negative thoughts. (Challenges)

Cl: Okay. I'll try.

1365. Th: Susie. I want to have you try something right now. It may seem weird, but I think it may be good for everyone to try it. I want you to go first. I want you to imagine your father is sitting in that empty chair right there. Tell him what you want to say to him. (Empty Chair Technique)

Susie: Daddy, I'm sorry you aren't here. I love you and I miss you.

1366. Th: Johnny, your turn.

Johnny: Hi dad. I don't know. I guess I miss you. I just wish you didn't have to leave.

1367. Th: Mom.

Cl: Oh, okay, let's see. I really wish we didn't have to do this. But here we are. I miss you as well. But things are how they are. That's all.

1368. Th: It is really feeling heavy in here. I want to shift for a minute and have you all give each other some positive messages. Take the paper there in front of you, and put a piece of tape on it like this. Now have someone put it on your back like this. Okay good. Now take turns writing something happy and positive about each person on the paper. (Pat on the Back)

1369. Th: Okay good. Now read each one out loud.

[Family takes turns reading comments.]

1370. Th: Now I can see how happy and together you are right now. I want to have you try a little game for a moment. I want you to pretend that you are back to where you were earlier, kids, you blame mom and be mean to her about the divorce, mom you pretend to be really upset and hurt by it. Remember that this is only pretend. (Pretend Technique)

[Family acts this out.]

1371. Th: Okay, you are all having a good time pretending. Now I want to have you switch roles for a minute. Johnny, you are mom. Mom, you are Susie. Susie, you are Johnny. Okay, let's do it again. (Role Playing)

[Again, family acts this out.]

1372. Th: Okay, I can see that this is a lot of fun. What are you noticing while you are doing this? (Open Question)

Cl: I am noticing how much fun it is to pick on mom.

Susie: I like being Johnny—it's easy to start a fight.

Johnny: I don't like being mom—that isn't fun to get picked on so much.

1373. Th: Oh, okay. So, it sounds like we are all seeing things from someone else's view. Now I want you to go back and be yourself, but this time, be the opposite of how you normally would be. Johnny, you and Susie are to defend mom, and mom, you are to be carefree about it, let it roll off your back. (Role Reversal)

[The family struggles to do this task; they realize that to follow the therapist's suggestion means they can't have the argument.]

Cl: Hey, that was really tricky.

1374. Th: Okay, well let's take a few moments and try another tricky thing. I want you (looking at mom) to put the kids, the furniture, anything you want in the room here, into a sculpture of how you want the world to be in regard to this problem. Include yourself, your kids, your ex-husband, any other family members, friends, and others as you determine necessary. The last thing for this exercise is for you to do all of this without talking to me or the kids. (Sculpting)

1375. Th: Okay good. Now describe for us what this sculpture represents. (Sculpting)

Cl: Well. Over here the kids are really enjoying what they do. They are growing up strong and healthy and are okay. Here is my ex-husband. He has moved on with his life and as you can see, has his life in order. These represent our friends. They are not torn between us anymore; they are okay as well. And of course, I am this feather over here. Life is good here.

1376. Th: Kids, I wonder if you could both take some time each drawing a picture of you and your dad. Use these markers and paper and draw what you feel should be in the picture. (Serial Art Therapy)

1377. **Th:** Mom, while the kids are doing that, I want you to take some time and draw a picture that represents in some ways what you just sculpted. You will take this with you. In this picture I want you to draw a wheel that has lines on it that represent the closeness or distance that you feel to members of your family and your friends. (Wheel of Influence)

Cl: Okay, I think that about does it.

1378. **Th:** So, I see that you have some people very close to yourself in the center. Can you tell me about the relationship you have with each of them? (Wheel of Influence and Open Question)

Cl: Yeah. These are my kids of course, and no one is closer than them. Here is my mom and dad, sister and brother after them. And then a little farther away is my ex-husband. All of these names are friends and acquaintances.

1379. **Th:** So you still feel a closeness to your ex-husband. (Reframe and Interpretation)

Cl: Yeah, I thought of that as I was doing this. I do still have a strong connection with him at some level.

1380. **Th:** Once again I am going to say something about your nonverbals. I noticed that as you talked about this connection you have with your husband, you wrapped your arms around you as if giving a hug. (Providing Feedback)

1381. **Th:** I want you to expand on that, really give yourself a good long hug, hold yourself close. (Experimentation)

Cl: All right.

[Client continues to hug herself, begins to cry.]

1382. **Th:** You are hugging yourself, but I sense there is someone else there, who else are you hugging? (Closed Question)

Cl: My husband.

1383. **Th:** Tell me about what this hug represents. (Prompt)

Cl: I am hugging him for the last time, I am saying good-bye. But it never works. I can't say good-bye yet.

1384. **Th:** You still love and miss very much both your husband and the relationship you had with him. (Empathy)

Cl: Yes.

1385. **Th:** All right, we have come a long way today. I want to leave you with some homework to do.

Reader assignment: Here we ask you, the reader, to propose a homework assignment for the client.

CHAPTER 14

....

Intertwined
Interventions

Intertwined interventions occur when the therapist connects two or more skills in one sentence or statement. The therapist may combine a paraphrase with an open question, a summary with a closed question, or a confrontation with immediacy, to name only three of the myriad of possible combinations. The potential for adding breadth and depth to the discussion with these advanced skills is endless. These interventions provide both speed and clarity to the therapy session.

It is not possible to list or stratify each of the various combinations of skills that might be present in all of the possible intertwined interventions, so we arbitrarily chose several different variations to show the utility and power of (1) combining skills in a purposeful way, (2) building a new skill, and (3) sending a more therapeutic statement or question to the client. Intertwined interventions may also help the therapist anchor the last portion of the statement made in previous material. For example, sometimes it is too big of a swing to take what a client has said and reflect back the deeper meaning. However, anchoring the therapist's lead on what the client has already said, reflected in different words, helps to show the client how the therapist arrived at the notion he or she did. With this approach there is less chance of resistance to what the therapist is saying.

Cl = Client
Th = Therapist

PARAPHRASE AND CLOSED QUESTION

1386. **Cl:** It has been really difficult for me to express how I feel to the group.

   Th: I understand that you have had problems sharing yourself in group (Paraphrase), and I am interested. When have you been most comfortable talking about personal things with the group (Closed Question)?

PARAPHRASE, REFLECTION OF FEELING, AND REFLECTION OF MEANING

1387. **Cl:** Last night my parents got in a really bad fight. They were yelling and screaming and throwing things around the house. It was really bad. I was really afraid of what was going on.

   Th: Last night was terribly rough with your parents fighting (Paraphrase) . . . you were scared and upset (Reflection of Feeling) . . . you believe families should get along better (Reflection of Meaning).

PROVIDING FEEDBACK AND PARAPHRASE

1388. **Cl:** I think things are going pretty well right now. My grades are improving, and I may go out for the volleyball team.

   Th: I can see the smile on your face as you share (Providing Feedback) how well things are going right now (Paraphrase).

REFRAME AND LOGICAL CONSEQUENCES

1389. Cl: As you can see, my children are a bit of a handful. I am very lucky to have my mother around to help watch the kids. She is an angel.

Th: Both you and your mother work very hard to make sure the kids are okay (Reframe), and I wonder what the kids are learning from having you two parent them (Logical Consequences).

REFLECTION OF FEELING AND REFRAME

1390. Cl: I don't want to tell my parents about his drinking . . . they already don't like him, and that would be enough to have them hate him and maybe me forever.

Th: I hear you saying you are anxious about your parents finding out (Reflection of Feeling). It is a real strength of yours to want to protect your relationships (Reframe).

REFLECTION OF MEANING AND FOCUS ON EXCEPTIONS

1391. Cl: I was thinking about going to college, but I know that my parents won't be able to pay for it, so I think it is best to just keep working at the gas station. Maybe in a few years I can take a few classes. Anyhow, I don't think that I could get in. My friend had better grades than me and they turned her down.

Th: It sounds like adults have let you down a lot (Reflection of Meaning). Tell me about a time in your life when people didn't let you down (Focus on Exceptions).

PROCESS ILLUMINATION AND FORCED CHOICE QUESTION

1392. Cl: I've been pretty down this week. I mean, I guess it was an okay week, but I keep thinking I shouldn't have said that to my daughter. She is pretty young and she really gets upset when I correct her harshly. Like the time that we were shopping, maybe six or seven years ago. I corrected her in front of some of her friends and she went off on me right in the mall. She is pretty sensitive to my criticism.

Th: I noticed just then that our discussion moved from talking about you to talking about your daughter's problems or concerns (Process Illumination). Would you like to talk more about feeling "pretty down this week" or would you like to talk about something else in relation to yourself (Forced Choice Question)?

CLOSED QUESTION AND PARAPHRASE

1393. Cl: I'm really having a difficult time with things right now. My car just went back into the shop, I am swamped at work, you know, things are pretty bad right now.

Th: Who, among everyone you know, has hope that your life will improve from being difficult and hard to being easier?

SELF-DISCLOSURE, STRUCTURING, AND PROMPT

1394. Cl: I always seem to get myself into situations where other people are mad at me. Why do you think that is?

Th: I appreciate you wanting me to give you an answer (Self-disclosure), but in our work together, the answers must come from you (Structuring). Tell me more about people getting mad at you (Prompt).

REFLECTION OF FEELING, REFLECTION OF MEANING, REFRAME, AND METAPHOR

1395. Cl: My friends seem to all be getting married and having children. I am still going to school and trying to figure out what I want in life. It's just hard to see them so happy with their lives and not know where I am going.

Th: I hear you saying that you feel isolated (Reflection of Feeling), and that you believe you should have a clear life plan right now (Reflection of Meaning), and in my mind I see the tortoise crossing the finish line ahead of the hare (Reframed Metaphor).

CHAPTER 15

Practice Exercises

We provided the following practice exercises to aid you in integrating new and more advanced skills. Each example includes a short description of the scenario followed by several comments made by the client(s) (Cl) that require you to come up with a therapeutic response. Try to use skills from various chapters of the book.

Practice Exercise 1

The client is a thirty-two-year-old father of three children. He has been divorced for six years. He came to therapy for help with what he describes as "anger-management issues."

> **Cl:** I am really tired of having to come home every night and clean up all of the day's events before I get to relax. In fact, I don't even get to relax.

[Response 1]

> **Cl:** I wish that someone would pitch in around the house and do some of the things that they expect of me.

[Response 2]

> **Cl:** I know it sounds like all I do is complain, but really, is it that much to ask someone to pick up their dirty dishes and put them in the sink?

[Response 3]

> **Cl:** I mean, sometimes I feel like there are no other people in the world who do the things I do and go through the things I do all to help my children be happy. And they get to do what they want while I'm at home fixing dinner, cleaning up, and sweeping.

[Response 4]

> **Cl:** There have been very few times in my life that I can remember the family doing something for me, you know, like cleaning the house, or making sure the dinner is made one week. The only time I can remember is when I had a broken leg. They helped out some then.

[Response 5]

Write your response, label the skill or skills used, then indicate your purpose for saying what you said.

Response 1 _____

_____

_____

Response 2 _____

_____

_____

Response 3 _____

_____

_____

Response 4 _____

_____

_____

Response 5 _____

_____

_____

Practice Exercise 2

The client is an eighteen-year-old female in her senior year of high school. Her presenting problem is career indecision.

Cl: I have no idea where I want to go with my life.

[Response 6]

Cl: I don't know what I want to do for a living—that's a hard question.

[Response 7]

Cl: I think about going to college, going into the Air Force, going right out and getting a job.

[Response 8]

Cl: But what I really want to do is relax and enjoy myself.

[Response 9]

Cl: My parents are always on my case about "what are you gonna do with your life," and I say, "I don't know," and then they get mad and then we fight and I storm out of the house.

[Response 10]

Cl: That happens fairly regularly. They just don't get me or understand me . . . like they never had questions in their head.

[Response 11]

Response 6 _____

_____

_____

Response 7 _____

_____

_____

Response 8 _____

_____

_____

Response 9 _____

_____

_____

Response 10 _____

_____

_____

Response 11 _____

_____

_____

Practice Exercise 3

The clients in this session are members of a closed group that is in its second session. They range in age from fifteen to seventeen. The group was started to help students with issues related to poor grades.

Jim: What are we doing in group today?

[Response 12]

Paula: Who cares, at least we are out of class.

[Response 13]

Missy: I have something to talk about.

[Response 14]

Jim: Well what is it?

[Response 15]

Missy: I got into trouble last weekend.

[Response 16]

Jim: Doing what?

[Response 17]

Paula: Let me guess . . . smoking.

[Response 18]

Darius: Yeah, so did I. A bunch of us got in trouble.

[Response 19]

Response 12 _____

_____

_____

Response 13 _____

_____

_____

Response 14 _____

_____

_____

Response 15 _____

_____

_____

Response 16 _____

_____

_____

Response 17 _____

_____

_____

Response 18 _____

_____

_____

Response 19 _____

_____

_____

Practice Exercise 4

The clients in this session are a married couple both in their mid-forties.
They sought therapy due to problems in the relationship.

Kristen: We have tried everything we can think of to relight the
fire in our relationship. It just seems that the pilot light has
gone out. You know?

[Response 20]

I come home from work and am so tired. I can't even think
about what it would be like to have sex then. Romance? Forget
it! There aren't enough hours in the day.

[Response 21]

Tom: Yeah, I feel the same way—and sometimes, it is like when I
do want to fool around, she is too tired, has to do something
more important, or wants to go to bed and sleep. I don't know
what to do.

[Response 22]

Kristen: But really . . . do you really want to have sex after
working all day? Wouldn't you really rather just talk? Or
snuggle? I know what you want, but I really am too tired most
of the time.

[Response 23]

Response 20 _____

_____

_____

Response 21 _____

_____

_____

Response 22 _____

_____

_____

Response 23 _____

_____

_____

Practice Exercise 5

The clients in this closed group have been together for six sessions. The core topic for this group is the issue of grief and loss. The members range in age from twenty-two to forty-one.

Thom: I am really glad that we have this group to explore our feelings about losing someone.

[Response 24]

Don: I have been thinking a lot about my father . . . what he meant to me.

[Response 25]

Eldridge: I get mad when I start to think about how unfair it was that my wife and son were killed by that drunk driver.

[Response 26]

Yolanda: I feel like I am going to cry.

[Response 27]

Sedona: It is nice that we can share such deep emotions and thoughts with one another.

[Response 28]

Kevin: But is this what we are supposed to be doing? How does this help?

[Response 29]

Response 24 _____

_____

_____

Response 25 _____

_____

_____

Response 26 _____

_____

_____

Response 27 _____

_____

_____

Response 28 _____

_____

_____

Response 29 _____

_____

_____

Practice Exercise 6

The client is a fourteen-year-old male who was referred to you by the principal. He was involved in a verbal altercation with another student. The principal has reported to you that the client has been bullying students since the start of the school year.

Cl: Man that really made me mad today.

[Response 30]

Cl: When he said that about my friend I wanted to rip his head off.

[Response 31]

Cl: I don't care about getting detention, and my dad will say I did the right thing too.

[Response 32]

Cl: Nobody talks to me like that.

[Response 33]

Cl: You guys are all the same, I know you hate me.

[Response 34]

Response 30 _____

_____

_____

Response 31 _____

_____

_____

Response 32 _____

_____

_____

Response 33 _____

_____

_____

Response 34 _____

_____

_____

Practice Exercise 7

The client is a seventy-nine-year-old female in a nursing home. You were asked to meet with her after the staff noticed she was not eating and seemed to have very little energy. Her husband passed away approximately two years ago. She arrived at the home less than three months ago.

Cl: I don't know where to start.

[Response 35]

Cl: Do you ask me a question or something?

[Response 36] I really don't know what to say.

[Response 37]

Cl: Things are okay, I guess.

[Response 38]

   Yeah, everyone keeps asking me about John (deceased husband). They all think I am acting strange or something.

[Response 39]

Response 35 _____

_____

_____

Response 36 _____

_____

_____

Response 37 _____

_____

_____

Response 38 _____

_____

_____

Response 39 _____

_____

_____

Practice Exercise 8

The client is a fifty-year-old male who reports he has arrived for therapy at the request of his wife. He has been having trouble staying focused at work (construction supervisor). His youngest child left for college four months ago.

Cl: My wife said I should come to counseling because I don't know how to share my feelings with her.

[Response 40]

Cl: She thinks that I am mad about something all of the time.

[Response 41]

Cl: You know, like I come home from work and sit down to watch some TV and then she wants to know what is on my mind . . . what happened during the day.

[Response 42]

Cl: I really just want to relax, have a beer, and watch some TV.

[Response 43]

Cl: I don't want to rehash all of the day's events.

[Response 44]

Response 40 _____

_____

_____

Response 41 _____

_____

_____

Response 42 _____

_____

_____

Response 43 _____

_____

_____

Response 44 _____

_____

_____

Practice Exercise 9

The client is a thirty-two-year-old single female. She has been coming to therapy for the last year and has been in and out of therapy for the last twelve years. She is seeing you to help with her depression.

Cl: I got a call from my sister the other day and she said that she was thinking about having an abortion.

[Response 45]

Cl: I had an immediate response to that.

[Response 46]

Cl: You remember I told you about, well, about my decision when I was sixteen to have one.

[Response 47]

Cl: Anyhow, my sister thinks that this will be best for her.

[Response 48]

Cl: I can't seem to get her to understand that she is making a big mistake and will regret it for the rest of her life.

[Response 49]

Response 45 _____

_____

_____

Response 46 _____

_____

_____

Response 47 _____

_____

_____

Response 48 _____

_____

_____

Response 49 _____

_____

_____

Annotated References

The following books were utilized in the creation of the skills list, the definitions of skills, and their use within the transcript. The theories books were also reviewed in order to augment the descriptions of the theories.

Amundson, N. E., Harris-Bowlsbey, J., & Harris-Bowlsbey, S. G. (2005). *Essential elements of career counseling: Processes and techniques.* Upper Saddle River, NJ: Pearson Education. 167 pages.

> This brief yet powerful text offers the reader specific examples of using basic and advanced skills in the arena of career counseling. The authors provide case examples, dialogue between the therapist and client, and a sequential approach to providing effective and useful career counseling.

Ansbacher, H. L., & Ansbacher, R. R. (1956). *The individual psychology of Alfred Adler: A systematic presentation in selections from his writings.* New York: BasicBooks, Inc. 503 pages.

> This extensive text covers the original writings of Alfred Adler as edited by the Ansbachers. The editors add useful and significant interpretations and insights into the original writings throughout the text. This book is a must read for practitioners using the techniques and theory associated with Individual Psychology.

Baker, S. B., & Gerler Jr., E. R. (2004). *School counseling for the twenty-first century* (4th ed.). Upper Saddle River, NJ: Pearson Education. 444 pages.

> Although this text is primarily a book used for teaching the basic and advanced skills of school counseling, it includes an excellent chapter on therapeutic skills. This chapter covers several types of therapy used in school settings (talk therapy, play therapy, and group therapy). The authors provide several "transcribed" moments from a therapy session.

Brammer, L. M., Abrego, P. J., & Shostrom, E. L. (1993). *Therapeutic counseling and psychotherapy* (6th ed.). Boston: Allyn & Bacon. 402 pages.

> This book covers individual, group, and family therapy techniques along with theoretical orientations. The therapeutic relationship is discussed in relation to being effective and purposeful in clinical work. This comprehensive text covers both basic and advanced clinical skills.

Byrne, R. H. (1995). *Becoming a master counselor: Introduction to the profession.* Pacific Grove, CA: Brooks/Cole. 320 pages.

This well-written basic therapy skills book is anchored in cognitive and cognitive-behavioral approaches. There are a number of specific techniques offered in the text that appear in our text as well. The authors make a great effort to explain both the use of the techniques and the theory behind them. This book is a must have for those clinicians who are interested in using cognitive-behavioral models.

Cade, B., & O'Hanlon, W. H. (1993). *A brief guide to brief therapy.* New York: W.W. Norton & Company. 202 pages.

This book covers the origin and current trends (up to the early 1990s) related to brief therapy. In doing this, the authors provide a text that should be read by anyone practicing brief therapy. Written in a breezy yet highly professional manner, the guide provides the basic tenets of brief therapy and integrates them with specific cases and examples. The common examples provided in this book make it possible for practitioners to use this as a critical resource in their therapy library.

Capuzzi, D., & Gross, D. R. (1992). *Introduction to group counseling.* Denver, CO: Love Publishing. 366 pages.

This group text introduces readers to the basic components and skills associated with group therapy. The authors pay close attention to facilitating groups with special populations.

Capuzzi, D., & Gross, D. R. (2003). *Counseling and psychotherapy: Theories and interventions* (3d ed.). Upper Saddle River, NJ: Pearson Education. 500 pages.

This edited text covers the major therapeutic theories. Specific attention is paid to the goals of each theory base, and the authors of each chapter are clearly experts regarding the theory base they discuss. Also, each chapter includes a case example to help the reader envision the theory as it might be practiced.

Corey, G. (2004). *Theory and practice of group counseling* (6th ed.). Belmont, CA: Brooks/Cole. 522 pages.

In this group therapy book, the reader will find the major therapeutic theories as they are utilized in group therapy. The author does an excellent job of providing specific examples of techniques related to each theoretical approach. Further, this text provides the reader with both the basic assumptions of group as well as the advanced application of specific group models.

Cormier, S., & Cormier, B. (1998). *Interviewing strategies for helpers: Fundamental skills and cognitive behavioral approaches* (4th ed.). Pacific Grove, CA: Brooks/Cole. 681 pages.

This book offers many examples and information related to cognitive-behavioral therapy. The authors of this text spend more time than most in describing the use and understanding of nonverbal behavior. This critical component to the therapeutic relationship is described by the authors through both the language of the client and of the therapist. This text does an excellent job of offering the reader both the typical basic and advanced therapeutic skills found in Western culture and with meditation and relaxation exercises associated more with Eastern cultures.

Doyle, R. E. (1998). *Essential skills and strategies in the helping process.* Pacific Grove, CA: Brooks/Cole. 308 pages.

This book provides a basic introduction to communication skills utilized by helping professionals. Covering the areas of affective, cognitive, and performance-based interventions, the author provides both individual skill development exercises and focuses attention on depth of the therapeutic response.

Dyer, W. W., & Vriend, J. (1988). *Counseling techniques that work.* Alexandria, VA: American Association for Therapy and Development. 288 pages.

This book focuses on skills and techniques used by both therapists and supervisors. One of the book's major strengths is the inclusion of specific transcribed sessions with comments that anchor theory into practice. The authors present the major therapeutic skills in a linear fashion, moving the reader from initiating the session to termination. This book contains many therapy techniques and how they might be used in a session.

Gladding, S. T. (2004). *Counseling: A comprehensive profession* (5th ed.). Upper Saddle River, NJ: Pearson Education. 544 pages.

This introductory text provides the reader with an overview of many of the issues and premises discussed in Chapter 1 in our book. Further, the reader is given several chapters that highlight the major therapeutic theories, along with cases and examples of what actual therapy sometimes looks and sounds like.

Hackney, H. L., & Cormier, L. S. (1996). *The professional counselor: A process guide to helping* (3d ed.). Boston: Allyn & Bacon. 390 pages.

This text uses a unique way of including many of the aspects reflected in our text. The authors integrate theory and skills and sort them into different types of interventions (affective, cognitive, systemic behaviors). In doing this, the concept of individual theoretical constructs gives way to a more integrated and eclectic approach.

Hanna, S. M., & Brown, J. H. (1999). *The practice of family therapy: Key elements across models* (2d ed.). Belmont, CA: Wadsworth. 342 pages.

In this text, the major family therapy theories are reduced to rudimentary and easy-to-follow parts. This allows the reader to more fully organize his approach to using family techniques. Specifically, the authors provide easy-to-follow decision trees, case examples, flow charts, and transcribed parts of sessions.

Hutchins, D. E., & Cole, C. G. (1992). *Helping relationships and strategies* (2d ed.). Belmont, CA: Wadsworth. 308 pages.

> The authors accomplish their main goal of helping the reader understand and utilize an eclectic approach to therapy. Overall, this is an excellent text in reference to "doing" activities. The authors provide case studies, examples of responses, practice exercises, and role plays for experiential learning. One of the major strengths of this book is that it seamlessly moves the reader from the theoretical constructs to the actual practice of a technique or approach.

Ivey, A. E., & Ivey, M. B. (2003). *Intentional interviewing and counseling: Facilitating client development in a multicultural society* (5th ed.). Pacific Grove, CA: Brooks/Cole. 446 pages.

> Perhaps one of the most well-known techniques texts, this book provides both the specific techniques of therapy along with a theoretical approach to integration and utilization of the basic therapeutic skills. The reader is encouraged to develop his or her own personal style by practicing specific therapy skills in a structured and specific way. Throughout the text the authors give brief demonstrations of skills in action. Along with these examples are opportunities for the reader to actually practice what they are reading.

Ivey, A. E., Pederson, P. B., & Ivey, M. B. (2001). *Intentional group counseling: A microskills approach*. Belmont, CA: Wadsworth. 293 pages.

> Along with the uniqueness of the Microskills Model, the authors provide a wonderful transcription of a group session. This transcript anchors the basic skills presented throughout the book in practice. The text is extremely user-friendly and clearly written so as to allow the reader a chance to both study and start to use new group therapy techniques.

Landreth, G. L. (2002). *Play therapy: The art of the relationship* (2d ed.). New York: Brunner-Rutledge. 408 pages.

> This play therapy text offers the reader a plethora of ways to envision how to effectively create a therapeutic place for children. From activities and materials to a clear theoretical orientation, the author successfully guides the reader along the helping process. A unique feature of this book is that it offers clear answers for practitioners in cases where they wonder "what to do?"

Lauver, P., & Harvey, D. R. (1997). *The practical counselor: Elements of effective helping*. Pacific Grove, CA: Brooks/Cole. 277 pages.

> This text is filled with bits and pieces of transcribed clinical work. The authors do a good job of integrating a general theory for progression through therapy stages. Unique to this text is a number of forms to be used by therapists to help upgrade and augment their skills.

Ludin, R. W. (1989). *Alfred Adler's basic concepts and implications*. Munci, IN: Accelerated Press. 166 pages.

In this brief text covering Individual Psychology, the author places great emphasis on the techniques Adlerians use. This is done by giving the reader pragmatic and easy-to-follow suggestions for clinical work. Taking the vast array of Adlerian concepts and breaking them down to their basic parts, the author offers the reader a hands-on tool for integrating theory into practice.

Madanes, C. (1984). *Behind the one way mirror: Advances in the practice of strategic therapy.* San Francisco: Jossey-Bass. 196 pages.

This book is a must read for practitioners interested in developing their knowledge and skills in working with families. The author clearly and succinctly moves the reader from understanding the true nature of the problem to intervening through various and varied means with family members. Perhaps the greatest strength of this book in relation to skill development is the vast array of examples of what a therapist might say in relation to a case.

Minuchin, S., & Fishman, C. (1981). *Family therapy techniques.* Boston: President and Fellows of Harvard University. 303 pages.

This text is a critical book for the library of the family therapist. The theory and specific practice applications of using a family structure approach are highlighted. Written in an easy-to-follow format, the book successfully integrates transcribed sessions with useful explanations in the text. Of note is the emphasis the authors place on therapy as being much more than simply stringing together techniques.

Murdock, N. L. (2004). *Theories of counseling and psychotherapy: A case approach.* Upper Saddle River, NJ: Pearson Education. 527 pages.

The goal of this text is to combine therapy theory with actual practice. Throughout each chapter is a specific theory or theories, along with very specific prescriptions of how to use the theory in practice. In fact, for a theory book, the author pays much more attention than most to the how-to section than the actual language and comprehensive theoretical constructs. This is a somewhat new and seemingly very useful way of providing techniques, skills, theory, and application.

Myrick, R. D. (1997). *Developmental guidance and counseling: A practical approach* (3d ed.). Minneapolis: Educational Media Corporation. 406 pages.

This school therapy–based text offers several chapters that specifically address the role of the school therapist in providing either individual or group therapy. Though the information is somewhat general, the author does an excellent job of distilling various theoretical constructs down to very easy-to-follow nuggets.

Okun, B. F. (1997). *Effective helping: Interviewing and counseling techniques* (5th ed.). Pacific Grove, CA: Brooks/Cole. 309 pages.

This text amplifies the need for therapists to be very purposeful in their work. In doing this, the author pulls together good case examples with clear techniques while integrating both ethical and multicultural perspectives. The book is heavy with examples and clearly stated properties of effective therapy.

Sommers-Flanagan, J., & Sommers-Flanagan, R. (1993). *Foundations of therapeutic interviewing.* Boston: Allyn & Bacon. 306 pages.

This text takes the reader through the stages of the helping process from the initial phone call to the last contact. The book provides the reader with specific things to consider and examples of what to say. The reader will find many excellent examples of what a clinician might say in relation to a specific skill.

Sommers-Flanagan, J., & Sommers-Flanagan, R. (2004). *Counseling and psychotherapy theories in context and practice.* Hoboken, NJ: John Wiley & Sons. 529 pages.

This text provides a comprehensive overview of the main theories currently in use today. Going beyond most theory texts, the authors provide a rich exploration of how a clinician might operationalize a theory.

Thompson, C. L., & Rudolph, L. B. (1996). *Counseling children* (4th ed.). Pacific Grove, CA: Brooks/Cole. 633 pages.

This book is one of the most comprehensive texts regarding integration of therapeutic theories with work specific to children. The authors take a careful look at working with kids across different theories. A somewhat unique characteristic of this book is the emphasis the authors place on therapists having a strong skill set in working with children with special needs.

Webb, N. B. (1999). *Play therapy with children in crisis* (2d ed.). New York: Guilford Press. 506 pages.

With authors from various disciplines, this edited text describes helping profession techniques and includes case analysis for working with kids in crisis. Many of the chapters have well-written and easy-to-follow examples of cases practitioners might experience. This book presents many specific activities a therapist can use with a client. Further, the book offers structured strategies as they might appear from session to session.

Yalom, I. D. (1995). *The theory and practice of group psychotherapy* (4th ed.). New York: BasicBooks. 602 pages.

Perhaps one of the most comprehensive group books currently in print, this text offers practical theoretical constructs for effectively facilitating groups. The author gives clear descriptions of techniques and the philosophical underpinnings of his theory. A significant contribution by this book is the way in which the author incorporates how to actually use the skills he describes, especially in light of moments when the group is not running as smoothly as would be hoped.

Index
....

Note: Page numbers in **bold** indicate the primary page for techniques.

NOTES

NOTES

NOTES

NOTES